Contents

The Life of Charlotte Brontë		4
The Times of Charlotte Brontë		8
PART ONE	Childhood	13
PART TWO	Lowood School	22
PART THREE	Thornfield Hall	35
PART FOUR	A Mysterious Visitor	46
PART FIVE	Mr Rochester Proposes	56
PART SIX	The Wedding	65
PART SEVEN	New Friends	79
PART EIGHT	Jane Makes a Choice	87
PART NINE	Return to Thornfield	98
Dossiers	Victorian Schools	29
	Victorian Family Life	74
	Victorian Houses	106

INTERNET PROJECTS   33, 86

ACTIVITIES   12,18,27,34,42,52,61,70,83,94,104
AFTER READING   110

PET PET-style activities 12,18,19,21,28,34,43,52,53,54,61,62
70,73,76,78,94,96,97,104

T: GRADES 5/6 Trinity-style activities   27,54,64,85,95

The text is recorded in full.
These symbols indicate the beginning and end of the passages linked to the listening activities.

Charlotte Brontë (1850) by George Richmond.

The Life of Charlotte Brontë

Charlotte Brontë was born in Thornton, Yorkshire, in the north of England in 1816. She was the third daughter of Patrick Brontë, a clergyman,[1] and of Maria Branwell. The family moved to Haworth Parsonage[2] in North Yorkshire in 1800. The couple had five daughters and one son. When Charlotte's mother died in 1821, the children's aunt, Elizabeth Branwell, went to live with the family. The children had only each other for company. They all loved reading and they created a magical world of their own, based on the stories that they read. They took as a starting point their brother Branwell's toy soldiers, and they

1. **clergyman** : priest.
2. **parsonage** : house where the priest and his family live.

Charlotte Brontë

Jane Eyre

Adapted by **Andrea Shell**
Activities by **Stanley Roberts**
Illustrated by **Gianni De Conno**

Editor: Daniela Penzavalle
Design and art direction: Nadia Maestri
Computer graphics: Simona Corniola
Picture research: Laura Lagomarsino

© 2008   Black Cat Publishing,
          an imprint of Cideb Editrice, Genoa, Canterbury

First edition : July 2008

Picture credits:
Cideb Archive; By courtesy of the National Portrait Gallery, London: 4, 6; from the Picture Collection at Royal Holloway, University of London: 8; ROCHESTER FILM LTD. / Album: 29; © Fine Art photographic Library / CORBIS: 30; Harrogate Museums and Art Gallery, North Yorkshire: 74; © Leslie Garland Picture Library / Alamy: 106.

All rights reserved. No part of this book may be reproduced, stored in a retrieval system, or transmitted, in any form or by any means, electronic, mechanical, photocopying, recording or otherwise, without the written permission of the publisher.

We would be happy to receive your comments and suggestions, and give you any other information concerning our material.

www.blackcat-cideb.com
www.cideb.it

The Publisher is certified by

in compliance with the UNI EN ISO 9001:2000 standards for the activities of 'Design, production, distribution and sale of publishing products.' (certificate no. 04.953)

ISBN 978-88-530-0774-2   Book + CD

Printed in Italy by Litoprint, Genoa

invented their own fantasy lands, called Angria and Gondal. They wrote histories and newspapers for these imaginary countries.

In 1824, the four eldest girls were sent to a boarding school [1] at Cowan Bridge, which Charlotte later used as a model for Lowood School in *Jane Eyre*. The severe conditions at the school were partly responsible for the deaths of Charlotte's sisters, Elizabeth and Maria, who both died in the same year, 1825. Charlotte herself was never completely healthy after her difficult time as a pupil at the school.

Charlotte was much happier at her second school, Roe Head. There she made one or two friends, who appeared in her novels in various forms. She later returned to the school as a teacher. She was, for a short time, governess [2] to two families, and then opened her own school at Haworth with her sister Emily (author of *Wuthering Heights*, published in 1847).

In 1842 Charlotte and Emily went to study languages at a school in Brussels, the Pensionnat Heger. During her stay, Charlotte fell deeply in love with Monsieur Heger, the director. He didn't return her love, and never replied to the letters that she sent him after she returned to Haworth. Charlotte later used this experience in her novel *Villette* (published in 1853).

Charlotte's first novel, *The Professor*, was not accepted by the publisher, but she then wrote *Jane Eyre*, which was a great success, and for which she is really famous.

Both Charlotte and her sisters, Anne and Emily, published their work under male pseudonyms, [3] as people did not respect women writers at that time. When the public realised that *Jane Eyre* was written by a

1. **boarding school** : school in which the pupils live during the school term.
2. **governess** : woman who taught small children privately.
3. **pseudonyms** : names which writers use instead of their real names.

The Brontë Sisters (about 1834) by their brother Patrick Branwell Brontë. From the left: Anne, Emily and Charlotte.

woman, some critics accused Jane of being coarse [1] and unfeminine. [2] Charlotte Brontë's family life was not happy. Her beloved sisters, Anne and Emily, both died while still young and her brother, Patrick, died of alcoholism after living an insignificant life. In 1854 she agreed to marry her father's curate, [3] Mr Nicholls, but the marriage was short-lived: Charlotte Brontë died in March 1855, at the age of thirty-nine, of an illness connected with childbirth.

Jane Eyre intrigues and gives pleasure to modern readers as much as it did when it was first published in 1847.

1. **coarse** : vulgar, unrefined.
2. **unfeminine** : with qualities not typical of women.
3. **curate** : assistant to the priest.

1 Comprehension check

Fill in the dates in the following sentences, then put them in the correct order to have a chronology of Charlotte Brontë's life.

1. ☐ Elizabeth and Maria both died in ....
2. ☐ Charlotte fell in love with Monsieur Heger in ....
3. ☐ Charlotte died in March, ...
4. ☐ Charlotte was born in ....
5. ☐ *Villette* was published in ....
6. ☐ Charlotte and Emily went to Brussels to study languages in ....
7. ☐ Charlotte went to boarding school with her three sisters in ....
8. ☐ *Jane Eyre* was published in ....
9. ☐ Charlotte married Mr Nicholls, a curate, in ....

2 Answer the following questions.

1. Who were Charlotte Brontë's parents?
2. How did the Brontë children play together?
3. What did Charlotte use as a model for Lowood School?
4. What experience did Charlotte write about in her novel *Villette*?
5. Why did the Brontë sisters use men's names to publish their works?
6. Why did Charlotte's marriage to Mr Nicholls not last?

3 Reading pictures

1. Look at the portrait on page 6. Write down three adjectives to describe the sisters, then compare your ideas in groups.
2. Which portrait of Charlotte do you prefer, the one on page 6 or the one on page 4? Why?

A detail from **The Railway Station** (1862), by William Powell Frith.

The Times of
Charlotte Brontë

Charlotte Brontë was born at a time of great change in Britain. Although she died at the young age of thirty-nine, she lived through the reigns of four monarchs. The last of these was Queen Victoria, who became queen in 1837. During this time, Britain was a rich and very strong nation. It had many industries, great writers and artists and a large empire.

This was the great age of the railways. Their rise was rapid and changed the lives of many people who had previously been unable to travel far from home. Roads were dangerous and uncomfortable to travel on by horse and carriage, especially in bad weather.

As industry grew and the railways opened up the country, people moved from the countryside into the big cities such as London, Manchester, Birmingham and Glasgow to find work.

There were many rich families in Britain at this time. Some were landowners who owned great estates. [1] Others were owners of factories and mines, who made their money from the new, growing industries.

For poor people, life could be very hard. There was little help if you had no job or friends to help you. There were diseases like cholera because of poor living conditions. There were revolts against unfair taxes and against new machines which deprived people of their jobs.

Most people during Charlotte Brontë's time had strong religious beliefs. Marriage and church-going were thought to be very important. Divorce was almost unknown.

In *Jane Eyre,* Charlotte Brontë used some of her own experiences of life and love and also reflected on some of the injustices of her time. Orphaned children often had a terrible life in institutions such as Lowood School. They were half-starved, [2] cold and easily became sick with diseases such as cholera. You may know the story of *Oliver Twist* by Charles Dickens (1838), in which Oliver is brought up in an orphanage even worse than the one described in *Jane Eyre.*

1 Reading pictures

Compare the scene in the painting on page 8 with what you see at a modern airport. What is different and what is similar?

1. **estates** : large areas of land.
2. **half-starved** : not given enough to eat.

2 Comprehension check
Decide if the following statements are true (T) or false (F). Correct the false ones.

		T	F
1	Very little happened in Britain during Charlotte Brontë's life.	☐	☐
2	The railways were replaced by major roads in this period.	☐	☐
3	Many people left agriculture to work in industry.	☐	☐
4	The poor did not fight against their bad conditions.	☐	☐
5	Religious institutions became a minor part of most people's lives.	☐	☐
6	*Jane Eyre* is, in part, autobiographical.	☐	☐
7	Children without parents received a lot of help from the government.	☐	☐
8	Charles Dickens also wrote about the suffering of young children.	☐	☐

3 Match the sentences A-D with the sentences 1-4.

A ☐ Britain was a prosperous nation.
B ☐ Travelling was difficult because roads were dangerous and uncomfortable.
C ☐ People began moving into the big cities.
D ☐ Life was very hard for the poor.

1 They lived in poor conditions and there were a lot of diseases.
2 It had many industries.
3 This was due to the railways which opened up the country.
4 The rise of the railways made people more mobile.

The Characters

A C T I V I T I E S

Before you read

1 Reading pictures
Look at the picture on page 15 and discuss these questions.

1 Who are the people in the picture?
2 Where are they?
3 What do you think is going to happen next?

2 Listening
Listen to the first part of Part One. You will hear about Jane Eyre's childhood. For each question, fill in the missing information. There is an example at the beginning (0).

Jane Eyre's Childhood

Cousins

0 Jane's cousins were never ..kind................ to her.
1 Jane was never happy because John .... her.
2 Jane escaped from her cousins in ....
3 John decided to .... because he had nothing interesting to do.

A bad girl

4 John Reed hit Jane because she took ....
5 John became angrier because Jane called him ....
6 John called his mother after Jane ....
7 John's mother thought that her son was .... to Jane.

12

PART ONE

Childhood

My name is Jane Eyre and my story really begins when I was ten years old. I was living with my aunt, Mrs Reed, because my mother and father were both dead. Mrs Reed was very rich and her house was large and beautiful, but I was not happy there. My three cousins, Eliza, John and Georgiana, were older than me. They teased[1] me, and never wanted to play with me. Sometimes they were very cruel. I was afraid of them.

Most of all, I was afraid of John Reed. He liked to frighten me and he made me very unhappy. I often hid from him in a small room. I liked to look at the pictures in the big books from the library there.

I felt happy and safe in my little room that day, because I knew that John and his sisters were with their mother. But then John got bored and decided to look for me.

---

1. **teased** : deliberately annoyed and embarrassed.

Jane Eyre

'Where's Jane Eyre?' he shouted. I kept very quiet and hoped he would not find me, as he was not a clever boy. But his sister Eliza soon found where I was hiding.

'Here she is,' she called, and I had to come out. John grinned [1] unpleasantly when he saw me.

'What do you want?' I asked him.

He made me stand in front of him. He stared [2] at me for a long time, and then, suddenly, he hit me. 'Now go and stand by the door,' he said.

Now I was really frightened. I knew that John was going to hurt me.

I went and stood near the door.

'I'll teach you to take our property,' said John Reed, and he picked up a large, heavy book.

At first I didn't know what he was going to do. Then he lifted his arm and I realised that he was going to throw the book at me. I tried to get out of the way, but I was too late. He threw the book straight at me; it hit me on the head, and I fell.

'You wicked [3] and cruel boy,' I shouted. 'Why do you want to hurt me?' I touched my head. There was blood on it. 'Look what you have done!' I cried.

My words just made John Reed angrier. He ran across the room towards me, and began to hit me again and again. I was very frightened, so I hit him back.

I don't know what I did to John Reed, but it hurt him. He started to call for his mother.

1. **grinned** : smiled.
2. **stared** : looked for a long time.
3. **wicked** : very bad.

Jane Eyre

'Mother! Mother!'

Mrs Reed heard the noise and hurried into the room. She didn't seem to see the blood which ran down my face.

'Jane Eyre, you are a bad girl!' she cried. 'Why are you hitting poor John, who is always so good to you?'

No one listened when I tried to say what John had done to me. Mrs Reed told two servants [1] to take me away.

'Take her to the red room and lock the door,' she told them.

The red room was cold and dark. A servant had told me that Mrs Reed's husband had died in the room. Nobody ever went there at night.

I was very frightened. I cried for help, but nobody came. 'Please help me!' I shouted. 'Don't leave me here alone!'

Nobody came. I cried for a long time. I was more terrified with every minute that went by. Then everything suddenly went black, and I think that I fainted. I remembered nothing after that.

When I woke up, I was in my own bed. My head was hurting. The doctor was sitting beside the bed. I felt very glad that someone who was not part of the Reed family was in the room with me. 'What happened to me?' I asked him.

'You are ill, Jane,' the doctor answered. 'The servant says that you have cried a lot. Why did you cry so much?'

'I cry because I am miserable,' I replied.

The doctor looked puzzled. [2] 'What made her ill yesterday?' he asked the servant.

1. **servants** : people who are paid to work in a house.
2. **puzzled** : confused, unable to understand.

Childhood

'She fell, sir,' was the reply. I could not waste this opportunity. I wanted the doctor to know the truth about my life with Mrs Reed and my cousins. 'I was knocked down,' I said. 'But that did not make me ill. I was shut up in a dark, cold room until after dark.'[1]

The doctor sent the servant away, and then he asked me, 'Are you unhappy here with your aunt and cousins?'

'Yes, I am,' I told him. 'I'm very unhappy.'

The doctor looked at me kindly. 'I see,' he said. 'Would you like to go away to school?'

'Oh yes, I think that I would,' I answered.

The doctor looked at me again for a long time, and then went downstairs to speak to Mrs Reed. Much later, Mrs Reed came to see me and told me that she had decided to send me to school.

A few days later, I left my aunt's house to go to school. I knew that Mrs Reed and my cousins were glad[2] to see me leave. They did not want me to go back for holidays. I had lived with them for as long as I could remember, but I was not really sad to leave. 'Perhaps I'll be happy at school,' I thought. 'Maybe there will be someone who likes me. I could find some friends there.'

1. **after dark** : night time.
2. **glad** : happy.

ACTIVITIES

The text and **beyond**

PET 1 Comprehension check

For questions 1-6, choose the correct answer — A, B, C or D.

1   Why did Jane Eyre live with Mrs Reed?
    A ☐ Because she liked her.
    B ☐ Because she didn't like her own home.
    C ☐ Because her parents were dead.
    D ☐ Because she didn't have any brothers or sisters.

2   What were the names of Jane's cousins?
    A ☐ Eliza, George and Maria.
    B ☐ John, Eliza and Georgiana.
    C ☐ Joseph, Georgina and Lizzie.
    D ☐ Lisa, Jack and Georgia.

3   Why was Jane unhappy?
    A ☐ Because she couldn't go to school.
    B ☐ Because she was ill.
    C ☐ Because Mrs Reed and her children were cruel to her.
    D ☐ Because Mrs Reed was cruel to her.

4   What did John Reed do to Jane?
    A ☐ He locked her in a room.
    B ☐ He didn't give her any food.
    C ☐ He tore her book.
    D ☐ He hit her.

5   John Reed looked for Jane and then hit her because
    A ☐ he had nothing better to do.
    B ☐ Jane had his books.
    C ☐ Jane hit him.
    D ☐ his mother told him to do these things.

6   Jane became ill because
    A ☐ John Reed knocked her down.
    B ☐ she was always sad.
    C ☐ she spent a terrifying night in a cold closet.
    D ☐ she always read inside her room.

ACTIVITIES

PET 2 Fill in the gaps

Poor Jane has no family or friend to write to, so she has to write to her diary. Read the diary entry below and choose the correct word for each space. For each question, mark the letter next to the correct word — A, B, C or D.

> I am writing to you, dear diary, to (1) .... you that I am very unhappy. I do not like (2) .... here with Mrs Reed and (3) .... children. Mrs Reed, (4) .... is my aunt, does not like me and her children are often cruel to me. Here is what (5) .... yesterday. I was reading quietly in the library (6) .... my cousin, John, hit me (7) .... my head started to (8) .... Mrs Reed did not care that I was hurt. She (9) .... me in a cold, dark room. No (10) .... came near me all night. I hope that I will leave here soon.

1	A say	B tell	C speak	D told
2	A live	B living	C lived	D to live
3	A her	B their	C your	D his
4	A which	B that	C who	D whose
5	A has happened	B happened	C hapened	D happens
6	A when	B as	C but	D until
7	A as soon as	B until	C when	D if
8	A blood	B bled	C bleed	D bloody
9	A lock	B brought	C locked	D bring
10	A where	B thing	C time	D one

19

ACTIVITIES

3 Find the mistake!

The sentences below all contain a mistake. Sometimes the words are in the wrong order, sometimes a word is incorrect and sometimes a word is missing. Try and correct the sentences.

0   John Reed : Where Jane Eyre is?
    Where is Jane Eyre?

1   .... : Here is she.

2   .... : What you do want?

3   .... : Now go by and stand the door.

4   .... : You wicked and cool boy.

5   .... : Jane Eyre, you are bad girl.

6   .... : Take her to the red room and locked the door.

7   .... : Please help me! Don't live me here.

 Can you write in the name of the person who said the words above? Check by listening to the recording.

4 Adjectives

Put the letters in order and find the correct adjective to fill the gaps in the following sentences.

chri	ckdwie	ralge	ldoc	rakd	naltupnaseyl	lcuer

1 Mrs Reed was very ....
2 Her house was .... and beautiful.
3 My cousins were sometimes .... to me.
4 John grinned .... when he saw me.
5 'You .... and cruel boy!' I shouted.
6 The red room was .... and ....

20

ACTIVITIES

5 Discussion: bullies

Discuss the following in pairs or small groups and then share your ideas in class.

1 A person who likes hurting or frightening a person who is younger or smaller or weaker is called a bully. Sometimes you find bullies at school. How do you say 'bully' in your language?
2 Can the members of the Reed family be defined as 'bullies'?
3 Why do the members of the Reed family treat Jane so badly?

Before you read

1 Reading pictures

Look at the picture on page 25 and answer the questions.

1 Where is Jane?
2 How are the girls dressed?
3 What do think the school will be like?

2 Listening

Listen to the first part of Part Two and decide if each sentence is correct or incorrect. If it is correct, mark A. If it is not correct, mark B.

		A	B
1	Lowood School looked just like her aunt's house.	☐	☐
2	There were nearly twenty girls in the room.	☐	☐
3	Jane did not eat the bread.	☐	☐
4	Each girl had her own bed.	☐	☐
5	Jane had a very small breakfast the next day.	☐	☐
6	Miss Temple offered the students lunch.	☐	☐

21

PART **TWO**

Lowood School

I started my journey to Lowood School in January. The weather was cold, windy and rainy and it was dark when I arrived. Lowood School was very large, but it was very different from Mrs Reed's house. It was cold and forbidding.¹ A teacher took me into a wide, long room which was full of girls. There were about eighty of them. Their ages were from about nine to twenty. They all wore ugly brown dresses.

It was time for supper.² There was only water to drink and a small piece of bread to eat. I drank some water because I was thirsty, but I was too tired to eat anything. After supper I went upstairs to bed with the other girls. The teacher took me into a very large room with many beds in it. All the girls slept in this one room and there were two girls in every bed.

1. **forbidding** : frightening, not welcoming.
2. **supper** : small meal eaten in the evening.

Lowood School

It was very early when I woke up next morning. It was dark outside and the big room was very cold. We had to wash ourselves in ice-cold water, and then put on our brown dresses. Then we went downstairs to the classroom for the start of the early morning lessons.

I was very hungry and it seemed a long time before it was time for breakfast. There was a terrible smell of burnt food. All of the girls were hungry, but the food was too badly burnt for us to eat. We all left the dining room feeling cold and miserable.

Lessons began again at nine o'clock. I looked at the other girls and thought how strange they seemed in their ugly brown dresses. Some of the girls were almost young women, and the dresses looked even more odd [1] and out of place [2] on these big girls. I did not like the teachers. They seemed to be very strict and unfriendly.

Miss Temple, the head teacher, came in to see us at twelve o'clock. Her face was very pretty and she seemed to be kinder than the other teachers. 'I have something to say to you all,' she said. 'I know that you could not eat your breakfast this morning, so I have decided that you will have bread and cheese for lunch.' The other teachers looked surprised. 'I'll pay for this meal myself,' Miss Temple told us. The girls were all delighted [3].

After we had eaten our lunch, we went out into the garden. It was very cold and our brown school dresses were too thin [4] to keep us warm in the winter weather. Nearly all of the girls

---

1. **odd** : strange.
2. **out of place** : not right.
3. **delighted** : very happy.
4. **thin** : (here) light.

Jane Eyre

looked cold and unhappy. Some of them looked very ill. I walked around the garden and hoped that someone would speak to me, but no one did.

One girl was reading a book, and I decided to try to be friendly with her. 'Is your book interesting?' I asked.

'I like it,' she replied.

'Does Miss Temple own the school?' I asked.

'No, she doesn't,' the girl answered. 'A man called Mr Brocklehurst owns the school. He buys all our food and clothes.'

This girl was called Helen Burns. I liked her immediately, even though she was older than me. I knew that she would be my friend.

I asked Helen a lot of questions about the school. She told me that some of the girls were ill because they did not get enough to eat, and they were always cold. Mr Brocklehurst was not a generous man. He bought clothes for the girls which were not warm enough for the cold winter, and there was never enough food to eat. Only very strong girls could stay well when they had to live in these hard conditions.

In the spring of that year, many of the girls became ill. They had a disease which was infectious [1] and some of them died. Lessons stopped, and we girls who were well spent most of our time outside in the fields near the school. The weather was now warm and sunny, so it was a happy time for us. My friend, Helen Burns, was not with us. She was so ill that she had to stay in bed.

1. **infectious** : can be passed from one person to another.

Jane Eyre

Miss Temple moved Helen into her own room, and one evening I went to see her. I felt great sadness when I saw how thin she was, and how pale her face had become. When she spoke to me, her voice was so low that I had to lean [1] close to her to hear what she said.

'Jane,' she said, 'it's so good to see you. I want to say goodbye.'

'Why, Helen?' I asked her, 'Are you going away from here?'

'Yes, I am, Jane,' Helen replied. 'I'm going far away.'

I stayed with Helen through the night to comfort her, and in the morning I found that she had died.

As a result of so many pupils dying at the school, there was an inquiry [2] into the conditions which had caused the disease. When people knew about the poor food, the dirty water and light clothing which the children were given, they gave money to improve [3] the lives of the girls. Lowood School was a much happier and healthier place from that time on.

1. **lean** : move the top part of my body.
2. **inquiry** : an official investigation.
3. **improve** : get better.

ACTIVITIES

The text and **beyond**

1 Comprehension check
Put the following sentences in the correct order to make a summary of Part Two. The first has been done as an example.

A ☐ I did not like the teachers. They seemed to be very strict and unfriendly.
B [1] I started my journey to Lowood School in January.
C ☐ After we had eaten our lunch, we went into the garden.
D ☐ Miss Temple, the head teacher, came in to see us at twelve o'clock.
E ☐ This girl was called Helen Burns.
F ☐ It was very early when I woke up next morning.
G ☐ One girl was reading a book. I decided to try to be friendly with her.
H ☐ In the spring of that year, many of the girls became ill.
I ☐ I stayed with Helen through the night to comfort her, and in the morning I found that she had died.
J ☐ A teacher took me into a wide, long room which was full of girls.
K ☐ After supper, I went up to bed with the other girls.
L ☐ It was dark when I arrived at the school.

T: GRADE 6

2 Speaking: rules and regulations
Lowood school was a charity school paid for by Mr Brocklehurst. Talk about your school using the following questions to help you.

1 Where does the money for your school come from? From the state? Or from somewhere else?
2 How many hours are you at school? Are you allowed to go home for lunch?
3 Do you have to wear a uniform? Do you think all schools should have a uniform? Why/why not?

ACTIVITIES

PET 3 Fill in the gaps

Read the letter from Miss Temple to Mrs Reed and choose the correct word for each space. For each question, mark the correct letter — A, B, C or D. There is an example at the beginning (0).

Dear Mrs Reed,

I think that Lowood School is just perfect for your niece. I am certain that she (0) ..**C**........ become a very good little girl here. The teachers here are very capable. The girls study many interesting (1) .... such as French, English literature and history. Most of our students find jobs (2) .... teachers or governesses when they leave Lowood. The school is not (3) .... expensive. All the girls (4) .... the same brown dress. This (5) .... a lot of money. The food is good and healthy, (6) .... not too extravagant. Also here at Lowood we believe (7) .... discipline is very important. All our girls (8) .... to respect authority. Our reputation is excellent. (9) .... has ever said anything bad about our teachers. I think your nieces will be very happy (10) .... us.

Please let me know if there is anything else you need to know.

Yours sincerely,
Miss Temple
Headmistress

0	A may	B could	**C will**	D must
1	A materials	B topics	C areas	D subjects
2	A like	B in	C as	D similar
3	A much	B greatly	C very	D lot
4	A carry	B dress	C wear	D put
5	A keeps	B holds	C maintains	D saves
6	A but	B and	C also	D however
7	A how	B that	C why	D which
8	A study	B learn	C become	D get
9	A Nobody	B None	C Person	D Anybody
10	A by	B with	C at	D from

In this scene from Franco Zeffirelli's *Jane Eyre* (1996) Charlotte Gainsbourg as Jane teaches Adèle; you will read about Jane's new teaching job in the next chapter.

Victorian Schools

When Jane Eyre went to Lowood School, she was very unhappy at first. There was not enough food for the girls to eat, their clothes were not warm enough for the cold winter weather and the teachers were very strict. Not all schools at that time were as bad as Lowood, but life in a Victorian school was still very different from life in most modern schools.

There were schools for many years before Queen Victoria's time, but very few of these were for the children of poor parents. The great public schools,[1] such as Eton, Harrow and Rugby were expensive places for the children of rich parents. There were also the old

---

1. **public schools** : (in Britain only) private schools.

The Naughty School Children by the French painter Theophile E. Duverger (1821-86). The little girls are punished by being humiliated.

grammar schools,[1] many of them from the sixteenth century. These schools were for the sons of merchants and other rich families who had enough money to pay the fees. William Shakespeare, who was born in 1564, was a pupil at the grammar school in Stratford-upon-Avon.

Many children of rich families did not go to school. They were taught at home by a governess or tutor in a special school room.

There were few schools for girls. Usually girls had to learn at home how to look after a house, how to cook and how to sew.

There were many children who had no time for learning at all. They had to work in factories[2] from a very young age. Some of the

1. **grammar schools** : schools for clever children.
2. **factories** : buildings where machines are used to make large quantities of goods.

churches started schools so that poor children could learn to read and write, and learn about religion. In the time of Queen Victoria, many more schools were started for poor children. In 1880 a law was made which said that children aged five to ten must go to school.
It cost three pennies a week, but in 1891 it became free.
Many schools were now built, but they were very different from modern schools. There were 60 to 80 children in each class, with only one teacher and a helper to look after them. The teacher sat at a high desk so that he could watch all the children. He was very strict and hit the children with a cane [1] when they made a mistake.
At first, poor parents didn't like their children going to school instead of working to earn money for the family. When builders came to put up schools in poor areas, angry parents often chased them away. [2]

1 Comprehension check

For questions 1-7, choose the correct answer — A, B or C.

1   All Victorian schools used to be
    A ☐ bad, with strict teachers and not enough food
    B ☐ very similar to modern schools
    C ☐ generally different from modern schools

2   What was a public school?
    A ☐ a school paid for by the government
    B ☐ a private school
    C ☐ a school for anyone

1. **cane** :
2. **chased them away** : forced them to go away.

3   What was a grammar school?
    A ☐ a school which only taught grammar
    B ☐ a school for poor children
    C ☐ a school for specially chosen children

4   Who taught children of rich families who didn't go to school?
    A ☐ their mother
    B ☐ governesses and tutors
    C ☐ servants

5   A law passed in 1880 said that
    A ☐ all children must go to school.
    B ☐ children should go to school if their parents agreed.
    C ☐ all children between the ages of five and thirteen must go to school.

6   Why did the teacher sit at a high desk in a Victorian classroom?
    A ☐ Because he could see all of the children.
    B ☐ Because he was not very tall.
    C ☐ Because he didn't like standing up.

7   Why did angry parents chase away the builders who came to put up the new schools?
    A ☐ They didn't want their children to learn to read and write.
    B ☐ They wanted their children to earn money for the family.
    C ☐ They didn't like new buildings.

INTERNET PROJECT

To find out more about schools in Victorian England connect to the Internet and go to www.blackcat-cideb.com or www.cideb.it. Insert the title or part of the title of the book into our search engine. Open the page for *Jane Eyre*. Click on the Internet project link. Go down the page until you find the title of this book and click on the relevant links for this project.

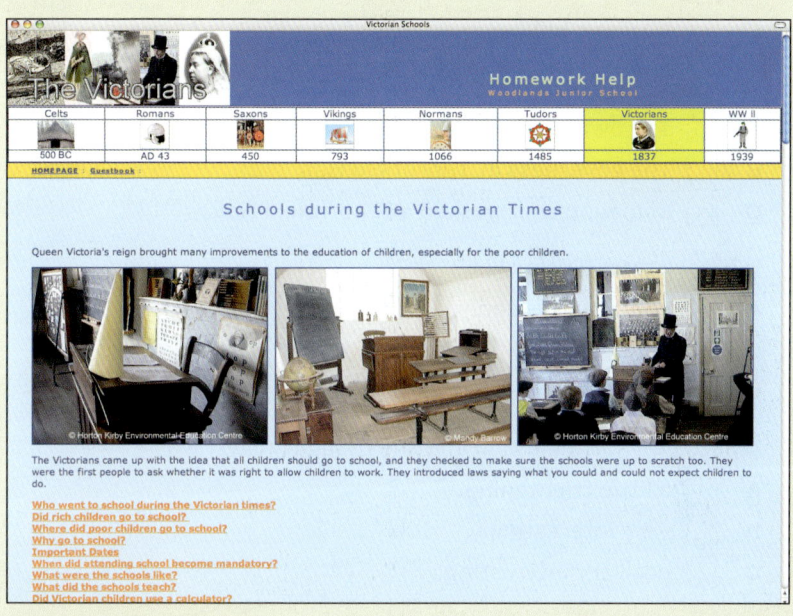

With your partner make a short report on one of these aspects of school in Victorian times.

- punishment
- games and sports
- slates
- abacuses
- classrooms
- subjects taught – the '3 Rs'
- teachers.

ACTIVITIES

Before you read

1 Listening

Listen to the first part of Part Three. For questions 1-6, choose the best answer — A, B or C.

1   When Jane got her first job she was
    A   [ ]   19 years old.
    B   [ ]   18 years old.
    C   [ ]   20 years old.

2   Who was Mrs Fairfax?
    A   [ ]   The owner of Thornfield Hall.
    B   [ ]   The governess at Thornfield Hall.
    C   [ ]   Someone who worked at Thornfield Hall.

3   What was Mrs Fairfax like?
    A   [ ]   young and friendly.
    B   [ ]   old and friendly.
    C   [ ]   old and unfriendly.

4   Jane liked Thornfield Hall and she thought that it was
    A   [ ]   a little frightening.
    B   [ ]   very interesting.
    C   [ ]   not very interesting.

5   The stranger fell off his horse because
    A   [ ]   the horse ran too quickly.
    B   [ ]   the horse jumped suddenly.
    C   [ ]   the horse fell on the ice.

6   What did the stranger ask Jane to do for him?
    A   [ ]   Hold his horse.
    B   [ ]   Get some help.
    C   [ ]   Move out of his way.

PART **THREE**

Thornfield Hall

I stayed at the school until I was eighteen, and for the last two years I was a teacher. I then decided that I wanted to see more of the world, and so I advertised in a newspaper for a job.

In my advertisement, I said that I was a young teacher who wanted to work as a governess to a family. I waited a long time for an answer. Then, at last, I received a letter from a lady, Mrs Fairfax, who lived at a place called Thornfield Hall. She wanted a governess for a little girl. I packed all my things into a small bag, and set out to start a new life.

I was very excited when I first saw the house in which I was going to work. It was very large, but it seemed very quiet. Mrs Fairfax was waiting for me at the door. She was an old lady with a kind face.

'I am pleased to see you, Miss Eyre,' said Mrs Fairfax. 'You must be tired after such a long journey. Sit down and rest. You will meet Adèle later.'

Jane Eyre

'Is Adèle my student?' I asked.

'Yes, she is nine years old. She is a little French girl, and Mr Rochester wants you to teach her English.'

'Who is Mr Rochester?' I asked.

'Mr Rochester owns Thornfield,' she replied. 'I only work here. I am the housekeeper.' [1]

'Where is Mr Rochester now?' I asked.

'He is away,' she said. 'He does not come very often to Thornfield. I never know when he will return.'

Next day I met Adèle. She was a very pretty little girl and at first I talked to her in French. I began to teach her English and I was glad that she enjoyed her lessons. I liked Adèle and I liked Mrs Fairfax, too. I was happy at Thornfield, although it was very quiet. Sometimes I was a little bored, but everyone was very kind to me.

One afternoon I walked to the village to post a letter for Mrs Fairfax. It was winter and the weather was very cold. There was ice on the road. As I walked back to Thornfield Hall, I heard the sound of a horse on the road behind me. I stood aside [2] to let the horse go past. The rider did not see me. He was a stranger with dark hair. Suddenly the horse slipped and fell down on the ice. The man was lying in the road. As I ran forward to help, he struggled [3] to get up.

'Are you hurt, sir?' I asked.

For a moment, the stranger was not able to answer me. Then he looked at me in surprise.

1. **housekeeper** : this person's job is to look after a house.
2. **aside** : (here) on the side of the road.
3. **struggled** : tried very hard.

Thornfield Hall

'Can I do anything to help?' I asked again.

'You can stand on one side while I catch my horse,' he replied.

But the horse managed to get up by itself, and I realised that it was the stranger himself who was hurt. He tried to stand up, but his injured leg was hurting too much. I helped him to get back onto his horse, and he rode away without thanking me.

'Who is he?' I asked myself. 'He is not very handsome and not at all polite, but he looks interesting. I would like to know him.'

When I arrived back at Thornfield, everyone was very excited and busy. I asked Mrs Fairfax what was happening.

'Mr Rochester has returned,' she said. 'But he may go away again soon. He wants to see you and Adèle, Miss Eyre. Go and put on your best dress. He will see you after dinner.'

After dinner, I took Adèle to see Mr Rochester in his room. When I entered the room, I stopped in surprise and stared at the man who was sitting in the chair. It was the man who had fallen from his horse. The interesting stranger was Mr Rochester!

Mr Rochester decided to stay at Thornfield for a while.[1] He was busy all day, but sometimes he talked to me in the evening. He did not smile or laugh very often, but he was an interesting man, and I was happy when I was with him. I liked my life at Thornfield Hall.

One night, long after[2] I had gone to bed, I woke up suddenly. It was very early in the morning. I thought that I heard something unusual. Everything was silent, but I listened very carefully, and I heard the sound again. Someone was moving about outside my room.

1. **a while** : some time.
2. **long after** : a long time after.

'Is anyone there?' I called. There was no answer. I felt worried and very frightened. But the house was silent again, and after a while, I tried to go back to sleep. But then I heard a laugh. It was a terrible, cruel sound, which made me quite cold with fear.

There was a sound of footsteps walking away, and going up the steps to the attic.[1] I could not sleep after that. I put on my

1. **attic** : a room at the top of a house.

clothes and went to find Mrs Fairfax. I heard nothing now, but suddenly I realised that I could smell smoke. It was coming from Mr Rochester's bedroom. I ran into the room and saw that his bed was on fire. I tried to wake him, but he did not move. I looked around the room, looking for something to put out the fire.

I saw a large jug[1] of water on a small table. I picked it up and

1. **jug** : container for water.

Jane Eyre

threw the water onto the burning bed. Then, Mr Rochester woke up.

'What's happening?' he cried. 'Is that you, Jane? What is wrong?'

'You must get up, Mr Rochester,' I said. 'Your bed was on fire, but I have put it out [1] now.'

He got out of bed quickly. The water was everywhere and there was still smoke from the fire.

'Jane, you have saved my life,' he said. 'What made you wake up? How did you know about the fire?'

I told him about the noise I had heard outside my room and the strange laugh.

Mr Rochester looked upset and angry. 'I must go upstairs to the attic,' he told me. 'Stay here and wait for me. Do not leave the room. Don't tell anyone what has happened.'

I waited in the room for a long time. At last, Mr Rochester came back. 'Go back to bed now, Jane,' he said. 'Everything is all right. You are quite safe.'

Next day, I asked Mrs Fairfax, 'Who lives in the attic?'

'A woman called Grace Poole,' she answered. 'She is one of the servants. She's a little strange.'

I remembered Grace Poole. She was a large, silent woman who did not speak to the other servants in the house. Perhaps it was Grace Poole who wandered [2] around the house at night, and laughed outside my door?

In the evening, when Adèle had finished her lessons, I went to talk to Mrs Fairfax.

1. **put it out** : extinguished it.
2. **wandered** : moved around without any clear direction.

Thornfield Hall

'Mr Rochester left the house early today,' she told me. 'He says that he is going to stay with friends. He didn't say when he will come back.'

The house was very quiet while he was away. Mr Rochester stayed with his friends for a few weeks, and I continued to teach Adèle her lessons. I did not hear the strange laugh again.

When I returned from a walk one day, I found that Mrs Fairfax and the servants were very excited. Mrs Fairfax showed me a letter which she had received from Mr Rochester. 'He is coming back tomorrow,' she said. 'He is bringing some of his friends with him. We are going to be very busy with so many visitors in the house. Miss Blanche Ingram is coming, too. She is very beautiful and very rich.'

Mr Rochester and his friends arrived the next day. Mrs Fairfax was right when she said that Miss Ingram was beautiful. But she was proud[1] too, and didn't seem to notice me.

I was too poor and unimportant. But she was very interested in Mr Rochester. They talked a lot together, and often went horse-riding.

'I think that Mr Rochester might marry Miss Ingram,' I said to Mrs Fairfax.

---

1. **proud** : very pleased with herself; she thought she was better than other people.

ACTIVITIES

The text and **beyond**

❶ Comprehension check
Answer the following questions.

1. Who was waiting for Jane when she arrived at Thornfield Hall?
2. What was the name of Jane's student?
3. What happened when she was coming home from the village one day?
4. What did the man look like?
5. What did Jane discover when she got home?
6. What did Jane hear when she woke up one night?
7. What did Jane see when she went to Mr Rochester's room?
8. What was the name of the woman whom Mrs Fairfax said lived in the attic?
9. Mr Rochester went away from Thornfield for a few weeks. Who did he bring with him when he returned?

❷ Discussion
Discuss the following with a partner. Compare your ideas with the rest of the class.

1. Jane's life changed when she went to live at Thornfield Hall. How?
2. What do you think are Jane Eyre's feelings towards Mr Rochester?
3. What does she mean when she says, 'the house was very quiet while he was away'?
4. Why do you think Jane told Mrs Fairfax that Mr Rochester might marry Miss Ingram?

'I was happy at Thornfield, although it was very quiet.'

Look at these sentences with **although**:
Although *many critics did not like* Jane Eyre, *it was a very popular book.*
(= *Many critics did not like* Jane Eyre, *but it was a very popular book.*)
Although *Jane was a small, plain woman, she was very courageous.*
(= *Jane was a small, plain woman, but she was very courageous.*)
Although is followed by a subject and a verb.
Clauses that begin with **although** are called 'clauses of concession'.

ACTIVITIES

3 Clauses of concession: although

Join the sentences using *although*. There is an example at the beginning (0).

0   Mr Rochester didn't thank her. / She helped him get back on the horse.
    Although she helped him get back on the horse, Mr Rochester didn't thank her.

1   Life was very difficult at Lowood. / Jane finished and became a teacher.
    ....

2   Jane's cousins and aunt were cruel to Jane. / She became a very kind woman.
    ....

3   Mr Rochester liked talking with her. / Jane was only a servant.
    ....

4   Jane did not wish to look for another job. / Many frightening things happened at Thornfield.
    ....

5   Mr Rochester didn't wake up. / His bed was on fire.
    ....

4 Listening

Look at the interview form. Some information is missing. You will hear part of a conversation about a job. For each question, fill in the missing information in the numbered spaces.

Name: (0) Jane Smith..

Position applied for: (1) ....

JOB EXPERIENCE

Worked in which kind of school: (2)........................

Length of time stayed: (3)......................................

Worked as: (4) ....

Name of employer: (5)...

When available: (6) ....

43

ACTIVITIES

5 How brave are you?

Jane Eyre was very brave when she saw and heard many mysterious things at Thornfield Hall. How brave are you? In pairs, ask each other the following questions.

1 If you woke up and heard terrible laughter, would you
 - A ☐ get up to see what was happening?
 - B ☐ call for help?
 - C ☐ hide under the bed?

2 If you found a small fire in the room, would you
 - A ☐ call the Fire Brigade?
 - B ☐ put out the fire yourself?
 - C ☐ run away and let someone else decide?

3 What would you do if you were left alone in a room when there was some sort of danger upstairs?
 - A ☐ go upstairs to find out what was happening?
 - B ☐ lock the door and wait for help?
 - C ☐ call your mother?

4 If someone had a bad accident in your house, would you
 - A ☐ try to help while you waited for the doctor?
 - B ☐ call the doctor, but not try to help because you might make things worse?
 - C ☐ keep away because you don't like to see blood?

5 When you are at home alone on a dark night, do you
 - A ☐ lock all the doors and windows, but go to bed at your usual time, and turn off the lights?
 - B ☐ stay up very late watching TV because you're scared to go to bed?
 - C ☐ hide under the table every time you hear a noise?

6 You are in bed, reading a book before you go to sleep. There is a large spider on the ceiling, above your bed. Do you
 - A ☐ ignore the spider, finish your book, and go to sleep?
 - B ☐ try to catch the spider and put it out of your room?
 - C ☐ scream for help?

ACTIVITIES

Check your answers with your partner.

Mostly A answers — You are very brave, but perhaps you should be a little more careful.

Mostly B answers — Quite brave, but also sensible. You think before you do things.

Mostly C answers — You need to try a bit harder. How about taking classes in self-defence or Kung-Fu?

Now discuss your answers with the rest of the class.

Before you read

1 Prediction

At the end of Part Three Jane tells Mrs Fairfax that she thinks Mr Rochester will marry Miss Ingram. What do you think?

2 Reading pictures

Look at the picture on page 47 and talk about these questions.

1 What time is it?
2 What do you think is happening?

Look at the picture on page 51 and talk about these questions.

1 Who is in this picture?
2 What do you think they are talking about?
3 How do you think they are feeling?

45

PART **FOUR**

A Mysterious Visitor

One evening, another visitor came to Thornfield Hall. He was a well-dressed young man with dark hair. He said that his name was Mr Mason and that he and Mr Rochester were old friends. But Mr Rochester looked alarmed [1] when he saw him. His face turned [2] white.

Mr Rochester and Mr Mason talked for a long time that night. They went to bed very late. I woke up suddenly and heard a terrible scream from the room above my bedroom. Then there was a lot of noise, as if people were fighting. There was another loud scream.

'Help!' I heard a voice shout. 'Rochester! Come quickly! Help me!'

I heard doors opening and the sound of someone running. I put on my clothes and opened my door. All the visitors were awake and standing outside their doors.

'What's happened?' they cried. 'Is there a fire? Who screamed?'

Mr Rochester came down the stairs from the attic. His friends

1. **alarmed** : afraid and worried.   2. **turned** : (here) became.

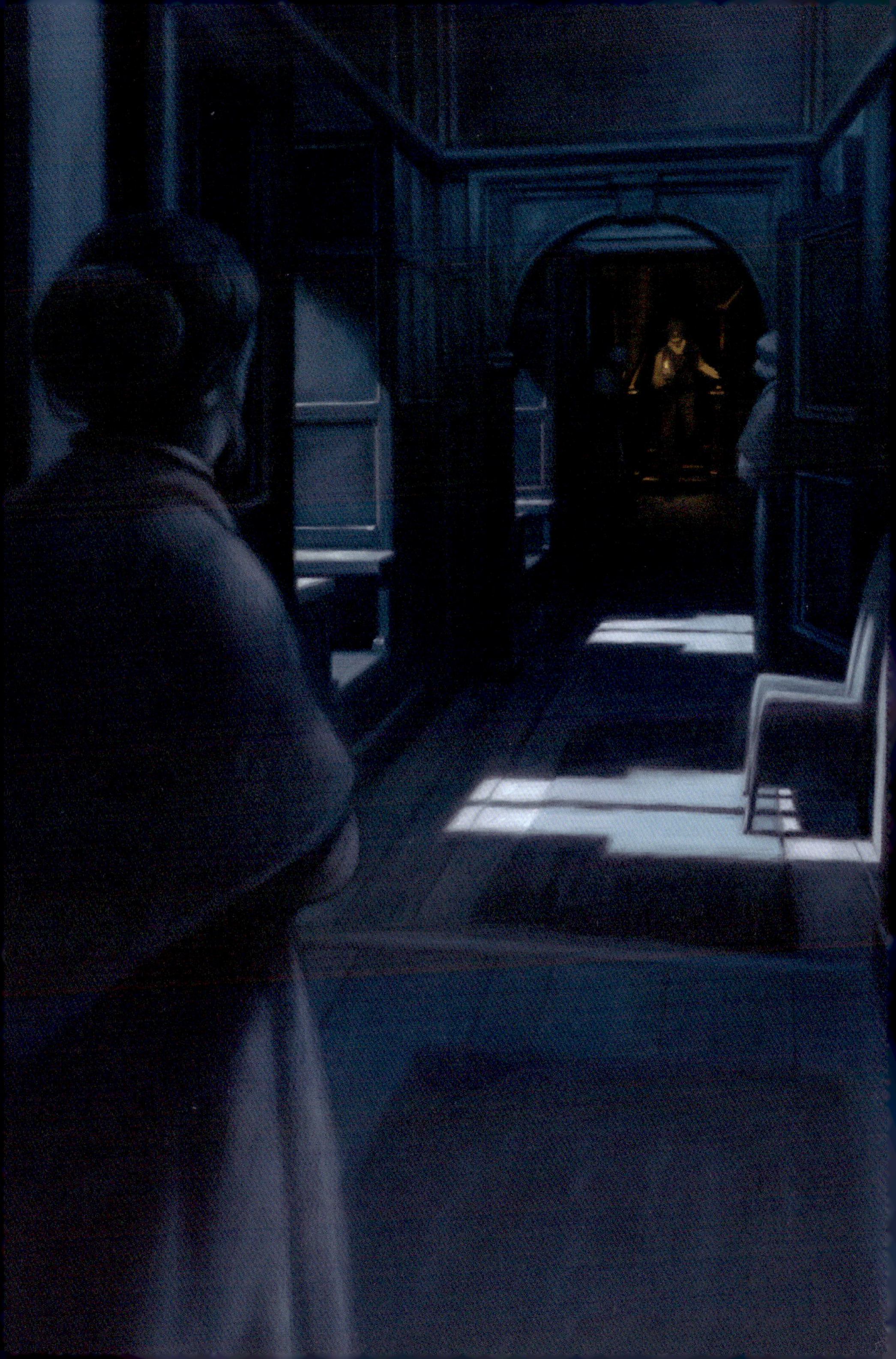

Jane Eyre

crowded around him, asking him questions. 'Everything is all right,' he told them.

'But what has happened?' someone asked.

'One of the servants had a nightmare, that is all. She's a very nervous person. She thought that she saw a ghost, and so she screamed. There is no need to worry. Please go back to bed now.'

One by one, Mr Rochester's friends went back to their rooms. I also went back to my room, but soon afterwards someone knocked at my door. I opened it and saw Mr Rochester.

'Jane, can you come with me?' he asked. I knew from his voice that something was very wrong.

'Yes, of course,' I said, and I followed him down the corridor and up the stairs to the attic. He unlocked the door of the attic and we entered the room.

'Wait here,' he said. I stayed outside the door of another room, while he unlocked it and went inside.

Then from behind this door I heard a terrible sound. It sounded like a wounded [1] animal, crying with rage. [2] Once again I heard that cruel, frightening laugh. Was Grace Poole inside that room? Mr Rochester came out and locked the door again. 'Are you afraid of the sight of blood, Jane?' he asked me.

'I don't think so,' I replied.

'Then come into the room with me,' he said.

I entered the room and saw that Mr Mason was lying on a

---

1. **wounded**: injured.
2. **rage** : great anger.

A Mysterious Visitor

large bed. His face was pale and his eyes were closed. His white shirt was covered in blood.

'Is he dead?' I asked.

'No,' Mr Rochester replied. 'He isn't badly hurt, but I must go and call a doctor for him. Will you stay with him until I return?'

Mr Mason moved and tried to speak. Mr Rochester said to him, 'Don't try to talk, Mason. You must not speak to Jane while I am away.'

Mr Rochester left me alone with the injured man. He was away for a long time and I was very frightened. Grace Poole was in the next room, and at any moment she might come in and try to hurt Mr Mason or me.

After a very long time, Mr Rochester came back with the doctor. Mr Rochester said to me, 'Thank you for your help, Jane. Mason is now going to leave Thornfield Hall. The doctor will take him away to be cared for in a safe place.'

I helped Mr Rochester and the doctor to get Mr Mason down the stairs and out of the house.

'Take care of him, doctor,' said Mr Rochester. 'Soon he will be well enough to go back to the West Indies.'

But before he got into the carriage, Mr Mason said something very strange. 'Look after her, Rochester. Promise to look after her.'

'Yes,' said Mr Rochester, and his face was very sad. 'I will always look after her.'

I wanted to go back to the house and to my bed, but Mr Rochester put his hand on my arm.

'Don't go yet,' he said. 'Walk with me for a while.'

Jane Eyre

We walked together in the garden.

'What a night that was,' Mr Rochester said. 'Were you afraid, Jane?'

'Yes, I was,' I replied. 'While I waited for you in the attic, I heard something in the next room... I heard a terrible laugh. Was it Grace Poole, Mr Rochester? Will she go away now?'

'Don't worry about Grace Poole,' he said. He did not look at me as he spoke. 'She will not harm[1] you. It is Mason I fear. I will not be happy until he is back in the West Indies.'

'But Mr Mason is a quiet and gentle man,' I said, surprised. 'I'm sure that he will do what you tell him.'

'No, he'll not hurt me deliberately,' Mr Rochester replied. 'But he might say something without meaning[2] to, which would do me great harm.'

I was surprised when I heard this. 'Then you must tell him to be careful about what he says,' I said.

Mr Rochester turned to look at me, and he laughed. 'It is not that simple, Jane,' he said. We went back into the house together.

---

1. **harm** : (here) cause physical injury.
2. **meaning** : (here) intending.

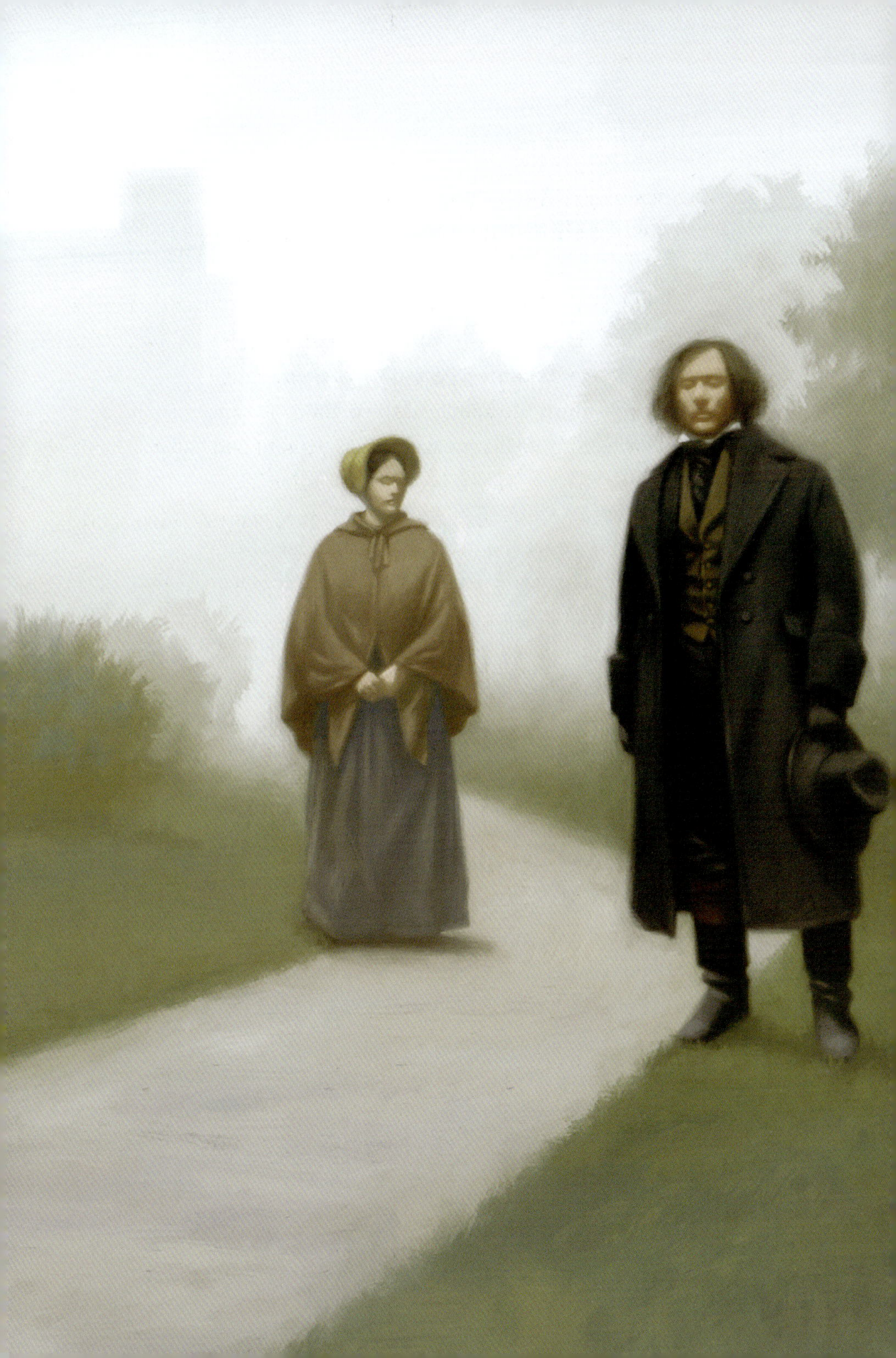

ACTIVITIES

The text and **beyond**

PET **1 Comprehension check**

Match the phrases in column A with those in column B to make true sentences. There are three phrases in column B that you do not need to use.

A

1. ☐ Mr Rochester became pale and frightened
2. ☐ Jane woke up in the middle of the night
3. ☐ Mr Rochester told his guests that his servant had had a nightmare
4. ☐ Mr Rochester came to Jane
5. ☐ Mr Rochester asked Jane if blood frightened her
6. ☐ Jane was very scared to stay alone with Mr Mason
7. ☐ Mr Rochester did not let Jane go back to her bed
8. ☐ Mr Rochester was afraid

B

A because Mr Mason had not yet left England.
B because he saw Mr Mason.
C because Grace Poole was in the next room.
D because he wanted to calm them down.
E because he heard the horrible cruel laugh.
F because he did not want to be alone.
G because he needed her to stay with an injured man.
H because he knew Grace Poole wanted to hurt her.
I because she heard a scream.
J because Mr Rochester knocked on her door.
K because he did not want Mr Mason to be alone.

52

ACTIVITIES

PET 2 Word building

Use the word given in brackets at the end of each sentence to form a word that fits in the space in the same line. There is an example at the beginning (0).

0 I like animals, but I ……..*feel*………….. nervous when I meet a big dog. (*feeling*)
1 In this game you don't kill the enemy, you ……………………… him. (*wounded*)
2 Please leave the door ……………………… . (*lock*)
3 He tried smiling at her so that he could hide his ……………………… . (*nervous*)
4 The fire was started ……………………… . (*deliberate*)
5 Help! Come ……………………… . (*quick*)
6 The room was very ……………………… . There were a lot of people shouting. (*crowd*)

3 Sentence transformation

For questions 1-8, complete the second sentence so that it means the same as the first, using no more than three words. There is an example at the beginning (0).

0 I received a letter from a lady.
   A lady …..*sent me*……. a letter.
1 He was a stranger.
   I ……………………… him.
2 You are quite safe.
   Nobody ……………………… you.
3 They went to bed very late.
   They did not go to bed ……………………… very late.
4 There is no need to worry.
   You ……………………… to worry.
5 Are you afraid of the sight of blood?
   Does the sight of blood ……………………… you?

53

ACTIVITIES

6   He was away for a long time.
    He did .... for a long time.
7   I will not be happy until he is back in the West Indies.
    I will only be happy .... he is back in the West Indies.
8   He'll not hurt me deliberately.
    He .... to hurt me.

T: GRADE 6

4 Speaking: travel

'Soon he will be well enough to go back to the West Indies.' In the time of *Jane Eyre* long distance travel was a long and difficult business. Talk about your experience of long distance travel, using the questions below to help you.

1   When you travel long distances which do you prefer: plane, train, coach, car or other? Why?
2   What do you do to pass the time on long journeys? Do you prefer to travel alone or in company? Why?
3   Have you ever travelled in an unusual way e.g. on an elephant, in a helicopter? Describe your experience.

Before you read

1 Listening

Listen to the first part of Part Five. For questions 1-7, choose the correct answer — A, B or C.

1   Mrs Reed's letter said that
    A ☐ she was dying.
    B ☐ John Reed was dead.
    C ☐ John Reed was dying.

2   Jane left to see her aunt
    A ☐ immediately.
    B ☐ after a few days.
    C ☐ after one week.

ACTIVITIES

3 Mrs Reed did not speak with Jane when she arrived because
   A ☐ she was angry with her.
   B ☐ she was not well.
   C ☐ she was very sad about her son's death.

4 Mrs Reed gave Jane a letter from
   A ☐ Mrs Reed's brother.
   B ☐ Jane's uncle.
   C ☐ Mrs Reed's father.

5 Mrs Reed gave Jane this letter
   A ☐ a few days after she received it.
   B ☐ a few years after she received it.
   C ☐ a few weeks after she received it.

6 Jane was happy
   A ☐ Mrs Reed died.
   B ☐ to leave Mrs Reed's house.
   C ☐ that she saw Mrs Reed again.

7 Jane thought
   A ☐ 'Maybe Adèle will not be happy to see me.'
   B ☐ 'I am certain Mr Rochester will be happy to see me'.
   C ☐ 'I am not certain Mr Rochester will be happy to see me.'

2 Prediction

In this part of the story you will read that Jane is going to leave Thornfield Hall. Why? With your partner choose one of the answers below or invent one of your own. Present your prediction to the class. What is the most common prediction?

A ☐ She wants a more interesting job.
B ☐ She wants to look for a husband.
C ☐ Mr Rochester is going to marry Miss Ingram.
D ☐ Mr Rochester asks Jane to marry, but she doesn't want to.
E ☐ Other ....

55

PART **FIVE**

Mr Rochester Proposes

Later that day, I received a letter which greatly surprised me. Mrs Reed, my aunt, was dying and she wanted me to go and visit her. I set off at once on a long journey to her home. When I got there, I was told that my cousin John had died. My aunt was very ill. At first she could not speak to me. But one day, as I was sitting by her bed, she showed me a letter. It was from my father's brother, who lived in Madeira[1]. This is what it said.

> Dear Mrs Reed,
> I am looking for my brother's daughter, Jane Eyre. I am now a rich man, and I have no children of my own. I want Jane Eyre to live with me. Can you help me to find my niece?
> Yours sincerely,
>
> John Eyre

1. **Madeira**: an island in the Atlantic Ocean off the north-west coast of Africa. It was a colony of Portugal.

Mr Rochester Proposes

I looked at the date on the letter. 'But, Mrs Reed,' I said, 'this letter was sent three years ago. Why didn't you tell me about it before?'

'I never liked you, Jane Eyre,' my aunt replied. 'I wrote a letter to your uncle and I told him that you were dead. I told him you died at Lowood School. Now go away and leave me.' A few days afterwards, Mrs Reed died. I felt sad that she had disliked me until her death, and I felt glad to leave her house and return to Thornfield Hall.

It was summer and the fields around Thornfield were very green and full of flowers. For me it was the most beautiful place in the world because it was now my home.

'I know that Adèle will be pleased to see me,' I thought. 'But what about Mr Rochester? I want to see him so much, but how does he feel about me? Perhaps he is already married to Blanche Ingram? What if they are going to marry soon? What will I do?' I felt unhappy when I thought about Mr Rochester and Blanche Ingram. 'I can't stay here when they are married,' I thought. 'I must leave this house, which I love, and I will never see Mr Rochester again.'

When I came near the house, I saw Mr Rochester. He was pleased to see me and so were Mrs Fairfax and Adèle. I really felt that I had come back home.

One evening, a few weeks afterwards, I went for a walk in the garden after I had finished teaching Adèle. Mr Rochester saw me there. 'Come and talk to me, Jane,' he said.

'He's going to tell me that he is going to marry Blanche Ingram,' I thought.

Jane Eyre

'Are you happy here, Jane?' he asked.

'Yes, Mr Rochester, I am very happy,' I replied.

'You'll be sad to leave here,' he said.

I could not look at him. 'He is going to tell me that I must leave because he's getting married,' I thought.

'Yes, I will be very sad to leave,' I said.

'But you must leave, Jane,' Mr Rochester said.

'Must I?' I asked. 'Will it be soon?'

'Yes, it will be soon,' he said.

'Is it because you are going to get married?' I asked.

'Yes, Jane, I am going to get married. Adèle must go to school and you must find a new job. I will help you. It will be far from here, though, my little friend.'

'Then I shall never see you again?' I cried.

'You'll soon forget me when you are far away,' he answered.

'But I will never forget you,' I thought. 'You may forget me, when I am not here, but I will never forget you, Mr Rochester.'

I could hardly speak. Tears were in my eyes and all that I could say was, 'Never!'

He looked at me for a long time and then, at last, he spoke. 'Perhaps you don't need to go,' he said. 'Perhaps you can stay here when I am married.'

I felt angry now. Did this man think I was made of stone? Did he not know how I felt? Did he even care how much his words hurt me?

'I could never stay,' I told him. 'When Miss Ingram is your wife, I must go. I know that I am not rich and beautiful like her. I am poor and unimportant. But I still feel sadness. If you marry Miss Ingram, I must leave here.'

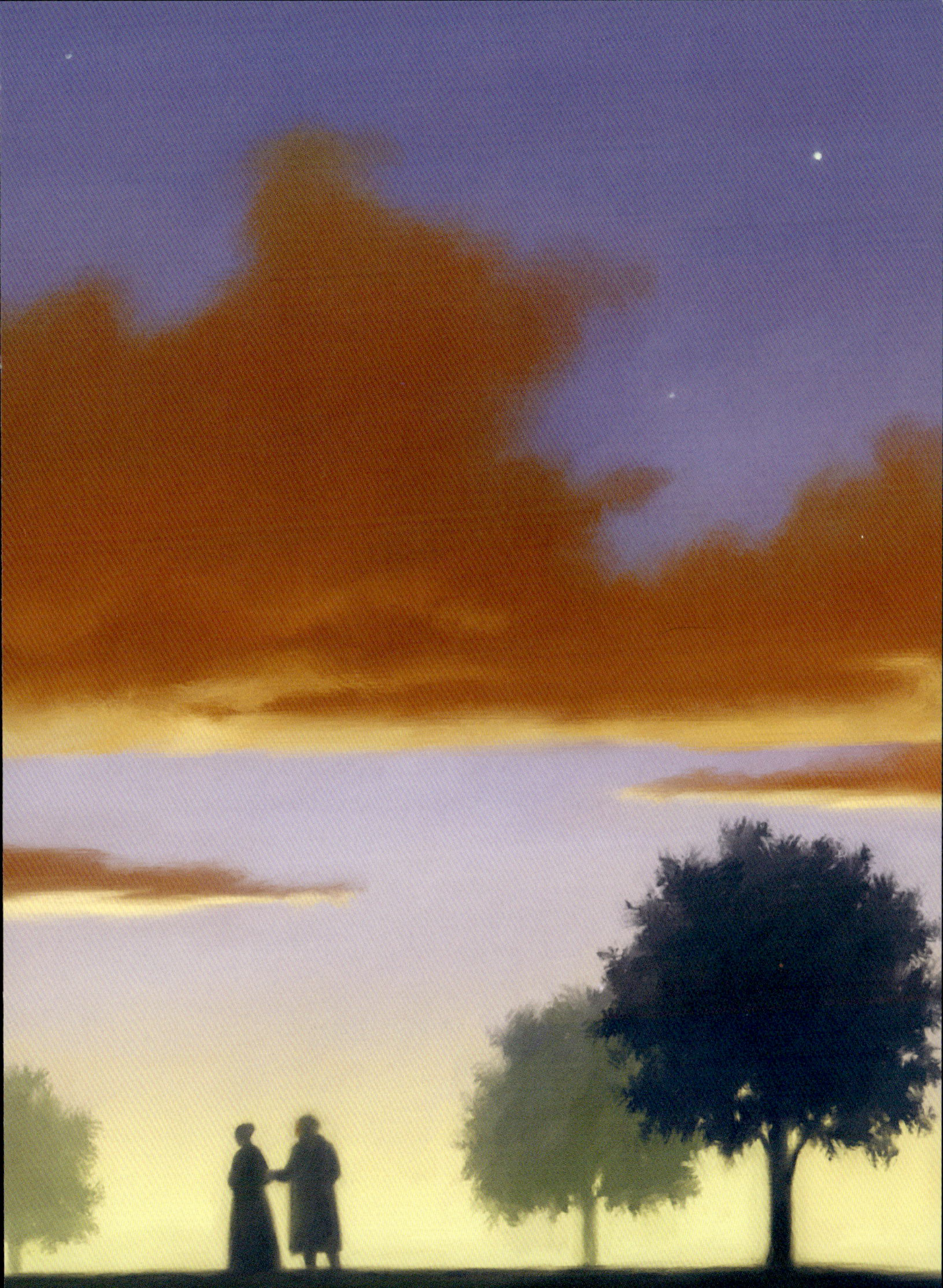

Jane Eyre

I was surprised when Mr Rochester smiled. 'But I don't want you to go, Jane,' he said. 'I am not going to marry Miss Ingram. Please stay here with me, because it's you I want to marry.'

I heard what he said but I could not believe it. 'You are laughing at me,' I said. 'How can you be so cruel?'

'I am not laughing at you, Jane,' he answered. 'It is you I want to marry, and not Miss Ingram. Jane, will you marry me?'

He looked at me so tenderly [1] that I had to believe him. Mr Rochester really did want to marry me! He wanted me, Jane Eyre, to be his wife!'

'Yes,' I said quietly, 'I will marry you.'

'We will be happy, Jane. No one is going to stop us,' he told me, with a strange look in his eyes, which I did not quite understand. But I was too happy at that moment to think about it for long.

It began to get dark. The weather changed and a strong wind started to blow. Rain started to fall as we walked back to the house together.

1. **tenderly** : with much love.

ACTIVITIES

The text and **beyond**

PET **1 Comprehension check**

Read these sentences about Part Five. Decide if each sentence is correct or incorrect. If it is correct, mark A. If it is incorrect, mark B.

		A	B
1	Jane's aunt was pleased to see her.	☐	☐
2	John Reed was dead.	☐	☐
3	Mrs Reed showed Jane a letter which she had received three days before.	☐	☐
4	Mrs Reed told Jane's uncle that Jane was in Madeira.	☐	☐
5	Jane was glad to leave her aunt's house.	☐	☐
6	Mr Rochester told Jane that she must find a new job.	☐	☐
7	Jane told Mr Rochester that she would soon forget him.	☐	☐
8	Mr Rochester asked Jane to be his wife.	☐	☐

Now correct the incorrect sentences.

2 What do you think?

Jane Eyre tells us that she has no money and that she is not very pretty. Mr Rochester is a rich man and is admired by many women. Here are some questions about Jane and Mr Rochester. Tick the answer that you think is the most probable.
There are no right or wrong answers. Discuss your ideas with the rest of your group.

1 Why do you think Mr Rochester wanted to marry Jane?
   - A ☐ Because she was beautiful.
   - B ☐ Because he thought she might have a lot of money.
   - C ☐ Because he loved her.

2 How will Jane's life change when she is married?
   - A ☐ She will go to many parties.
   - B ☐ She will live with someone who really cares for her.
   - C ☐ She will buy expensive clothes.

61

ACTIVITIES

3 Why might Jane be happy when she is married?
  A ☐ Because Mr Rochester loves her.
  B ☐ Because she can send Grace Poole away.
  C ☐ Because she won't have to work again.

4 Why might Jane be unhappy when she is married?
  A ☐ Because Mr Rochester is much older than she is.
  B ☐ Because she has no money of her own.
  C ☐ Because she might be bored because she doesn't have a job.

PET 3 Summary

Read the summary of parts 1-5 and choose the correct word — A, B, C or D. There is an example at the beginning (0).

At the beginning of the story Jane Eyre was ten years old and lived (**0**) ..A..... her aunt, Mrs Reed, and her three cousins, Eliza, John and Georgiana in a beautiful, big house. Both her parents (**1**) .... died.

Her cousins were cruel to her and one day John hit her. Jane was (**2**) .... to a cold and dark room where she became ill. The doctor asked her if she would like to go away to school.

Jane's first school was Lowood, owned (**3**) .... Mr Brocklehurst. He was an unkind man (**4**) .... did not buy enough food and clothes for the eighty girls that lived there. Jane made a very good friend at Lowood called Helen Burns who died because of the harsh conditions. (**5**) .... other girls died and so an inquiry was made. The government sent money to Lowood and the school improved.

Jane left Lowood when she (**6**) .... eighteen. She took a job (**7**) .... a French girl, Adèle, in a house called Thornfield Hall. One day when Jane was out in the village she saw an interesting looking man fall (**8**) .... his horse. She tried to help him but he refused. When she got back to Thornfield she discovered that the stranger was (**9**) .... employer Mr Rochester. One night Jane heard noises outside her room. She found Mr Rochester's bed on fire. He thanked her for saving his life and went up to the attic to investigate the strange noises.

Mrs Fairfax, the housekeeper, told Jane that a strange, quiet woman called Grace Poole lived upstairs.

One day, (**10**) .... visitor called Mr Mason came to Thornfield. Late that night Jane heard (**11**) .... from upstairs and found Mr Mason

ACTIVITIES

(12) .... on a large bed in the attic, covered in blood. Mr Rochester went to get a doctor. Mr Mason was taken away and Jane and Mr Rochester discussed Grace Poole. Mr Rochester seemed very worried.

Mrs Reed was dying. Jane went to see her and discovered that her uncle had (13) .... to contact her from Madeira. Mrs Reed had told him that Jane was dead. Jane returned to Thornfield and prepared (14) .... leave. She was sure that Mr Rochester wanted to marry a beautiful woman (15) .... Blanche Ingram. Instead Mr Rochester wanted to marry her. She accepted.

0	A (with)	B by	C at	D to
1	A have	B are	C had	D were
2	A took	B taken	C take	D taked
3	A at	B by	C for	D to
4	A that	B which	C who	D when
5	A Many	B Much	C Lot	D Few
6	A had	B has	C reach	D was
7	A teaches	B teaching	C teach	D taught
8	A to	B through	C across	D from
9	A his	B her	C its	D it's
10	A a	B an	C one	D the
11	A shoutings	B screamings	C scream	D screams
12	A lying	B laying	C laid	D lay
13	A tryed	B train	C tried	D trained
14	A for	B to	C a	D with
15	A call	B name	C called	D naming

'I really felt that I had come back home.'

When we are talking about the past we use the past simple. When something happened in the past before another thing, we use the **past perfect** for the first action and the past simple for the second action. The past perfect is formed with **had + past participle**.
Look at these sentences:
Mr Rochester left Thornfield on Tuesday. Jane arrived at Thornfield on Wednesday.
We can also rewrite them in this way:
*When Jane **arrived** at Thornfield, Mr Rochester **had** already **left**.*

63

ACTIVITIES

4 The past perfect

Read the text below about Charlotte Brontë's marriage. Put the verbs in brackets into the simple past or past perfect.

In 1852 the Reverend Arthur Nicholls (0) ..proposed.. (propose) marriage to Charlotte. Actually, Arthur (1) .... (fall) in love with her several years earlier, but he (2) .... (be) not a very brave man. Surprisingly she (3) .... (accept): before then she (4) .... (consider) him to be boring. Also, Charlotte still (5) .... (think) about the Belgian teacher she (6) .... (fall) in love with several years earlier. But Arthur's great passion for Charlotte (7) .... (convince) her. Fortunately for us, Charlotte (8) .... (write) her great novels before marrying Arthur. Once married, she (9) .... (write) that 'my time is not my own.'

T: GRADE 6

5 Speaking: special occasions

1 In Part Five Mr Rochester asks Jane Eyre to marry him. What do you think the wedding ceremony will be like?

2 Present a short report on traditional weddings in your country to the class. Bring a picture or two to help. Include some of the following ideas and information:
- who conducts the ceremony
- what the bride and groom wear
- other family members who are important in the ceremony
- when it is held
- the kind of festivities associated with the wedding — meal, music...

Before you read

1 Reading pictures

Look at the picture on page 69 and talk about these questions.

1 Describe the woman in the picture.
2 Who is she? What do you think is happening?

PART **SIX**

The Wedding

The wedding day was a month later. I was busy and happy as I got ready for the marriage.

Two nights before the wedding, I was asleep in my room. My wedding dress was in the room with me. The night was windy and the wind made a strange noise. Suddenly, I woke up. There was a light in my room. I thought at first that it was morning, but when I looked at the window I saw that it was still dark outside.

Someone was in my room. Was it Mrs Fairfax or Grace Poole? It was a woman, but a woman I had never seen before. She was big, tall and strong. Her black hair was long and thick. She was dressed in a long, white garment.[1] I could not see her face. She held my wedding dress and veil up in front of her. She looked at her reflection in the mirror and it was then that I saw her face! It was the most terrible face. She had large, red eyes and her skin was purple. She looked angry and dangerous. I felt great fear.

1. **garment** : (here) a long dress.

Jane Eyre

Then she took my veil and tore it to pieces [1]. She threw the pieces down on the floor and went over to look out of the window. Then she turned and started to come towards my bed. I was so frightened that I was unable to move. I couldn't even scream for help. 'She is going to kill me,' I thought. But then the light disappeared, and the room was dark once more.

I woke up in the morning. The sun was shining in through the window, and at once I remembered the strange woman. I thought at first that I had had a bad dream. Then I saw my ruined [2] veil, lying on the floor, torn to pieces. It was true! The strange woman was real!

Mr Rochester looked very worried and was silent for a long time when I told him about the woman, but he just said, 'You had a bad dream, Jane. It was probably Grace Poole who tore your veil, but you dreamt that it was a stranger.'

I could not believe that the strange woman had been just a dream, but I said nothing. That night, the night before the wedding, I slept in Adèle's room.

The next day, we went to the church for the wedding. In the church, while the clergyman was speaking, someone threw open the church door and said, 'Stop the wedding! It cannot go on. Mr Rochester already has a wife. He is married to my sister!'

All the people in the church turned to see who was speaking. It was Mr Mason, the visitor from the West Indies, with two other men. What was he talking about? How could Mr Rochester be married? My heart turned cold. I could not believe that this was happening on my wedding day.

1. **tore it to pieces** : ripped, pulled it into pieces.
2. **ruined** : so damaged it could not be repaired.

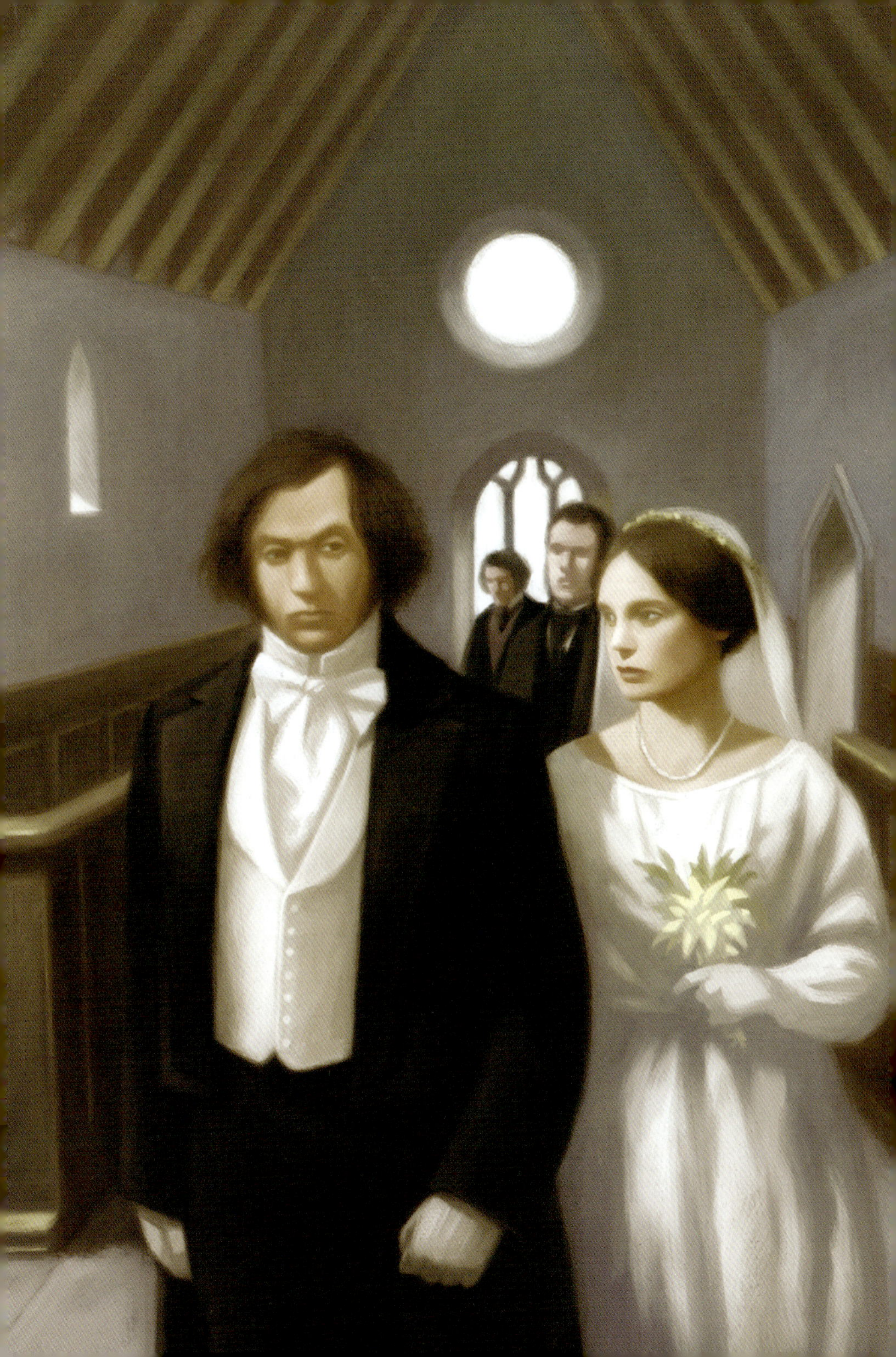

Jane Eyre

'But where is Mr Rochester's wife?' asked the clergyman. 'Why haven't we seen her?'

'She lives at Thornfield Hall,' Mr Mason replied. 'She is alive. I saw her recently.'

Mr Rochester struggled to speak. His face was white and distressed.[1] At last he said, 'It is true. My wife is living at Thornfield Hall. We were married fifteen years ago in the West Indies, when we were both young. Her name is Bertha Mason, and she is Mason's sister. Soon after we were married, she changed. She became very strange and then she became mad and dangerous. She attacked me and anyone who came near her. Last April, she tried to kill her own brother.

'She has a nurse, Grace Poole, who looks after her at Thornfield. I have told no one else that she is my wife. This young woman, Jane Eyre, knows nothing about her.' Mr Rochester's face was sad. 'Come with me and I will take you to see her.'

We were all silent as we walked from the church back to Thornfield Hall. Mr Rochester took us up to the attic and unlocked the door. Grace Poole was there, and in the room, too, was the frightening, terrible woman that I had seen in my bedroom. She was the person who had the cruel laugh. She was the one who had set fire to Mr Rochester's bed, who had tried to kill Mr Mason and who had ruined my veil. Yes, she was mad, but she was also Mr Rochester's wife. I knew that I could not marry him.

Although I felt sorry for Mr Rochester, I knew that I must leave my home, Thornfield Hall, for ever. I put a few clothes into a small bag. I took a little money, and quietly left Thornfield Hall early the next morning. I told no one that I was going, and no one saw me leave.

1. **distressed** : agitated, tormented.

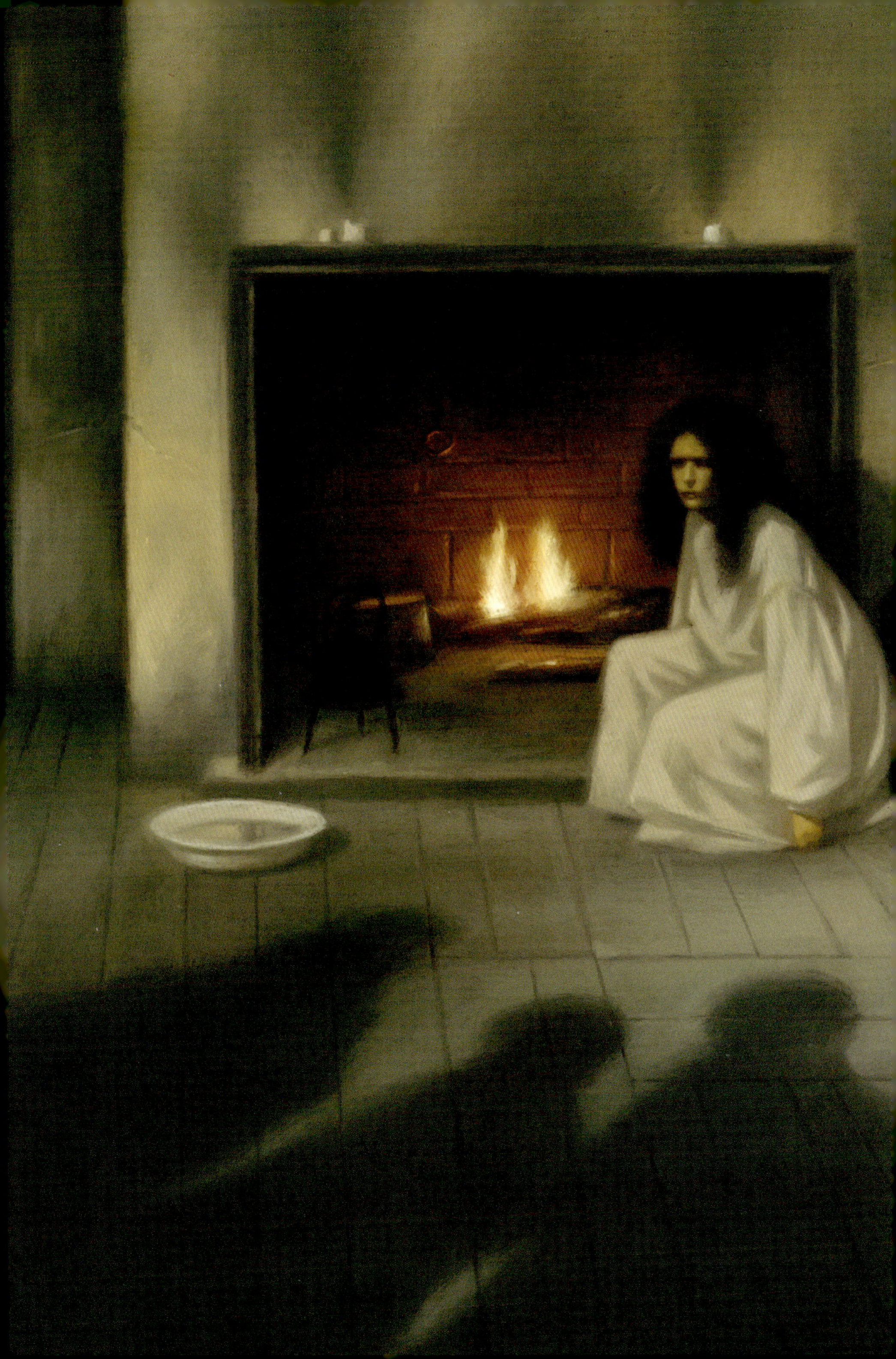

The text and **beyond**

PET **1 Comprehension check**

For questions 1-7 choose the correct answer — A, B, C or D.

1 What happened two nights before the wedding?
- A ☐ Mr Mason arrived at Thornfield.
- B ☐ Someone tore Jane's veil.
- C ☐ Mr Rochester went away.
- D ☐ Jane had a dream.

2 What did Mr Rochester say to Jane when she told him what had happened?
- A ☐ He said that it was a bad dream.
- B ☐ He told her not to be silly.
- C ☐ He said that he would buy her a new dress.
- D ☐ He told her she would get a new veil.

3 Who interrupted the wedding?
- A ☐ the clergyman
- B ☐ two men
- C ☐ Mr Mason
- D ☐ the priest

4 Mr Rochester couldn't marry Jane
- A ☐ because he forgot the ring.
- B ☐ because he was already married.
- C ☐ because he wanted to marry someone else.
- D ☐ because he didn't love her.

5 Who was Mr Rochester's wife?
- A ☐ Mr Mason's sister
- B ☐ Adèle's mother
- C ☐ Miss Ingram's friend
- D ☐ Mr Mason's sister-in-law

ACTIVITIES

6 Why was Mr Rochester's wife locked up in the attic?
   - A ☐ Because Mr Rochester didn't like her.
   - B ☐ Because Mr Rochester wanted to marry Jane.
   - C ☐ Because she was mad.
   - D ☐ Because she was shy.

7 Who looked after Mrs Rochester?
   - A ☐ Mrs Fairfax
   - B ☐ Mr Mason
   - C ☐ Grace Poole
   - D ☐ nobody

2 Summary

Here are six sentences from Part Six. Put them in the order in which they appear in the story.

- A ☐ Mr Rochester looked very worried and was silent for a long time when I told him about the woman.
- B ☐ 'But where is Mr Rochester's wife?' asked the clergyman. 'Why haven't we seen her?'
- C ☐ Although I felt sorry for Mr Rochester, I knew that I must leave my home, Thornfield Hall, for ever.
- D ☐ Then she took my veil, and tore it to pieces.
- E ☐ 'It is true. My wife is living at Thornfield Hall.'
- F ☐ Two nights before the wedding, I was asleep in my room.

Now, on your own or in pairs, choose one more sentence from Part Six to put in the summary above. Put it in the right place, then compare your choices in class.

ACTIVITIES

3 Vocabulary
Match the words (1-4) with their definitions (A-E). Use your dictionary to help you.

1 ☐ a dream   A pleasant thoughts that you have while you're awake
2 ☐ a nightmare   B an imaginary place
3 ☐ a daydream   C frightening or disturbing thoughts that you have while you sleep
4 ☐ a dream world   D what you imagine while you sleep

4 Discussion
Have you ever had a bad dream? Work in pairs and describe your dream to your partner. Take it in turns to describe your partner's dream to the rest of the class.

5 Find the mistake!
Correct the words that are underlined.

A You had a <u>good</u> .... dream.
   ....

B <u>Start</u> .... the wedding!
   ....

C But where is Mr Rochester's <u>husband</u> .... ?
   ....

D She is <u>dead</u> .... I saw her recently.
   ....

E It is <u>false</u> .... My wife is living at Thornfield Hall.
   ....

F She has a <u>doctor</u> ...., Grace Poole, who looks after her at Thornfield.
   ....

Now check your answers by listening to Part Six again. Write the name of the speaker in the space below the words.

ACTIVITIES

PET 6 Fill in the gaps

Read this report of Jane and Mr Rochester's wedding from the local newspaper. Choose the correct word (A, B, C or D) to fill in each space.

> ## Shock Ending to Wedding of Wealthy Local Man
>
> The wedding of wealthy Mr Rochester (1) .... Thornfield Hall to a member (2) .... his staff, Miss Jane Eyre, a governess, ended dramatically in the village church (3) .... week. Miss Eyre, (4) .... looked radiant in a dress of plain white satin, was (5) .... about to agree to marry the handsome, rich owner of Thornfield Hall, when (6) .... a stranger entered the church, and said that the marriage could not go (7) .... Mr Rochester and Miss Eyre then left the church, with their guests. Mr Rochester and Miss Eyre have not been (8) .... since the wedding.

1	A at	B of	C for	D to
2	A from	B of	C at	D on
3	A before	B next	C last	D since
4	A who	B that	C which	D were
5	A just	B only	C as soon as	D until
6	A quickly	B sudden	C quick	D suddenly
7	A on	B up	C down	D back
8	A saw	B see	C seen	D look

7 Writing

You are a journalist for the newspaper above (activity 6). Write an article (100-150 words) for the newspaper of the next day. Decide how much new information you know now, and what the readers of the newspaper will be interested in.

Many Happy Returns of the Day (1856) by William Powell Frith, an artist who specialised in scenes of Victorian society. This scene shows a birthday party.

Victorian Family Life

Charlotte Brontë was twenty-one when Queen Victoria took the throne. The story of *Jane Eyre* shows the importance that Victorians gave to marriage, family life and religion. When Jane discovers that Mr Rochester is already married, she knows immediately that they cannot be together, and that she must leave Thornfield for ever.

For rich families, family life was comfortable and pleasant. Servants were cheap and every family had at least one maid (a female servant). In a large house like Thornfield, there was probably a butler,[1] many maids, a cook and gardeners. Once the house was

---

1. **butler**: male head servant.

cleaned in the early morning, ready for when the family got up, the servants stayed 'downstairs' in the basement, until one of the family rang a bell to call them 'upstairs'.

The sons of the family had to work hard at school so that they could succeed in their careers, but young women had to learn social skills such as singing and playing the piano. The only 'career' for most well-off young women was a good marriage. Some poor girls with a better education sometimes worked as governesses or companions to older women. When a young man and woman liked each other, the man asked the girl's father for permission to visit her. The young couple could only meet if an older person was with them as a 'chaperone'.[1] After a while, the man would ask if he could marry the girl. Her father would ask him about his job, his money and his future plans before he would agree to the marriage.

The family followed a regular daily routine. Meals were at the same times each day, and children were told off[2] if they were late. They had to eat all their food. If they didn't, it would be there again at the next meal. In the evening in winter, children played indoor games. In summer they played in the garden.

Victorians liked inviting guests to their homes, and they gave large, expensive parties. During the summer months, most families went on holiday. Sometimes they went to the seaside and a few, very rich families went abroad to countries like France or Switzerland.

1. **chaperone** : older person who supervises someone younger.
2. **told off** : spoken to angrily.

PET 1 A diary entry

Imagine that you live in a rich Victorian family. Here is a page from your diary. Read the entry for 15 July 1841 and choose the correct word (A, B, C or D) to fill in each space.

Thursday, 15 July 1841

I got (**1**) .... at seven o'clock. A butler (**2**) .... me some hot water so that I could have a wash (**3**) .... my bedroom. At seven-thirty we (**4**) .... breakfast. I had bacon, eggs and a glass (**5**) .... milk. At eight-thirty I started lessons (**6**) .... my governess, Miss Eyre. At eleven-thirty we had our lunch and I (**7**) .... all my food. If I leave (**8**) ...., then Mama (**9**) .... make me eat it (**10**) .... the next meal. In the afternoon, it rained, so we stayed indoors and played games. (**11**) ...., when Papa came home, we sang songs while Mama played the piano. At eight o'clock I went to bed.

1	**A** up	**B** across	**C** along	**D** out
2	**A** bring	**B** took	**C** brought	**D** take
3	**A** on	**B** at	**C** for	**D** in
4	**A** have	**B** had	**C** having	**D** halve
5	**A** a	**B** of	**C** an	**D** some
6	**A** with	**B** by	**C** buy	**D** on
7	**A** eat	**B** eaten	**C** ate	**D** eats
8	**A** any	**B** many	**C** much	**D** some
9	**A** won't	**B** going	**C** will	**D** for
10	**A** for	**B** on	**C** at	**D** by
11	**A** After	**B** Before	**C** Between	**D** Later

2 A film scene

Work with a partner. Imagine you are actors. Take it in turns to be a Victorian father and the young man asking to marry his daughter. Here are some ideas for questions and answers.

Father: Are you sure that you love my daughter?

Young man: I love her with all my heart.

Father: You don't look old enough to be married. How old are you?

Young man: I'm twenty-one years old, sir.

Father: What kind of work do you do?

Young man: I work in a bank.

Father: Do you earn enough money to buy a house for my daughter?

Young man: No, sir, but my family will lend me the money.

Father: I want my daughter to live near her mother and me.

Young man: I don't want to take her away from her family, sir.

Now repeat the same scene according to the film director's instructions:

1 young, hippie father — very serious young man
2 young, athletic father — easy-going young man
3 old-fashioned, narrow-minded father — clever young man

3 Reading pictures

Look at the picture on page 74 and talk about these questions.

1 'Many happy returns of the day!' is the phrase people say to a person on his/her birthday. In the painting, whose birthday is it?
2 What elements of this scene do you think are typically Victorian?
3 What are the similarities and differences between the birthday party in the painting and the kind of birthday parties that you go to?

ACTIVITIES

Before you read

1 Listening

Listen to the first part of Part Seven. For questions 1-6, choose the correct answer — A, B or C.

1 Jane had no more money because
   A ☐ she had used it all to get away from Thornfield Hall.
   B ☐ she left Thornfield in a hurry and forgot it.
   C ☐ she lost it during her journey from Thornfield Hall.

2 Jane decided to ask for help in the house because
   A ☐ she saw some women eating inside.
   B ☐ the people inside seemed nice.
   C ☐ there was a servant inside.

3 Jane was told to leave the house
   A ☐ by the two young women.
   B ☐ by a serious young man.
   C ☐ by the servant.

4 Jane told the people a false name because she didn't want
   A ☐ her new friends to look for her house.
   B ☐ Mr Rochester to find her.
   C ☐ her new friends to know she had no family.

5 St John Rivers was
   A ☐ not very attractive.
   B ☐ very attractive.
   C ☐ very ugly.

6 The two young women were
   A ☐ more serious than their brother.
   B ☐ not as serious as their brother.
   C ☐ nicer than their brother.

78

PART **SEVEN**
New Friends

I wanted to travel as far away from Thornfield as I could, so I spent all my money on a journey which took two days and nights. I arrived at a place where there were no towns or villages. There were very few houses. I had no money and I was cold, tired and hungry.

It was dark now and I could see a light in the window of a house. I looked through the window. There were two young women in the room. I thought that they looked kind, so I knocked on the door. It was opened by a servant.

'Who are you?' she asked. 'What do you want?'

'I'm alone in the world and I have no money or food,' I told her. 'I'm tired and hungry. Please, can you help me?'

The servant stared at me. She did not look very friendly. 'I'll give you some bread,' she said. 'But then you must go. You can't stay here.' She came back and gave me the bread, and said, 'Now go away.'

Jane Eyre

But I was too tired to move. I sat down outside the door of the house. 'There is no one to help me,' I said. 'I will die here.'

I didn't know that someone was watching and listening to me.

'You are not going to die,' a voice said. A tall, handsome young man was looking down at me. 'Who are you?' He knocked on the door and the servant opened it again.

'Who is this young woman, Hannah?' he asked.

'I don't know, sir,' the servant replied. 'I gave her some bread and told her to go away.'

'She can't go away, Hannah,' the young man said. 'She is too ill. We must take her inside and help her.'

They took me into the house, where it was warm and comfortable. The two young women asked me my name. 'I am Jane Elliott,' I told them. I didn't want to tell them my real name in case Mr Rochester tried to find me. I wanted to start a new life.

My kind new friends took me upstairs to a bedroom, where I slept for a very long time. When I woke up, I felt much better.

I was soon well enough to talk to the people who had been so kind to me. The names of the two young women were Diana and Mary Rivers. The young man was their brother and his name was St John Rivers. He was a clergyman. He had fair hair and blue eyes and was very good looking. But his face was always serious and he did not often laugh or smile. He planned to go to India to work.

Diana and Mary were much friendlier than their brother, but I didn't want to tell them about Mr Rochester. 'I have no family of my own,' I said. 'My parents are dead. I went to Lowood

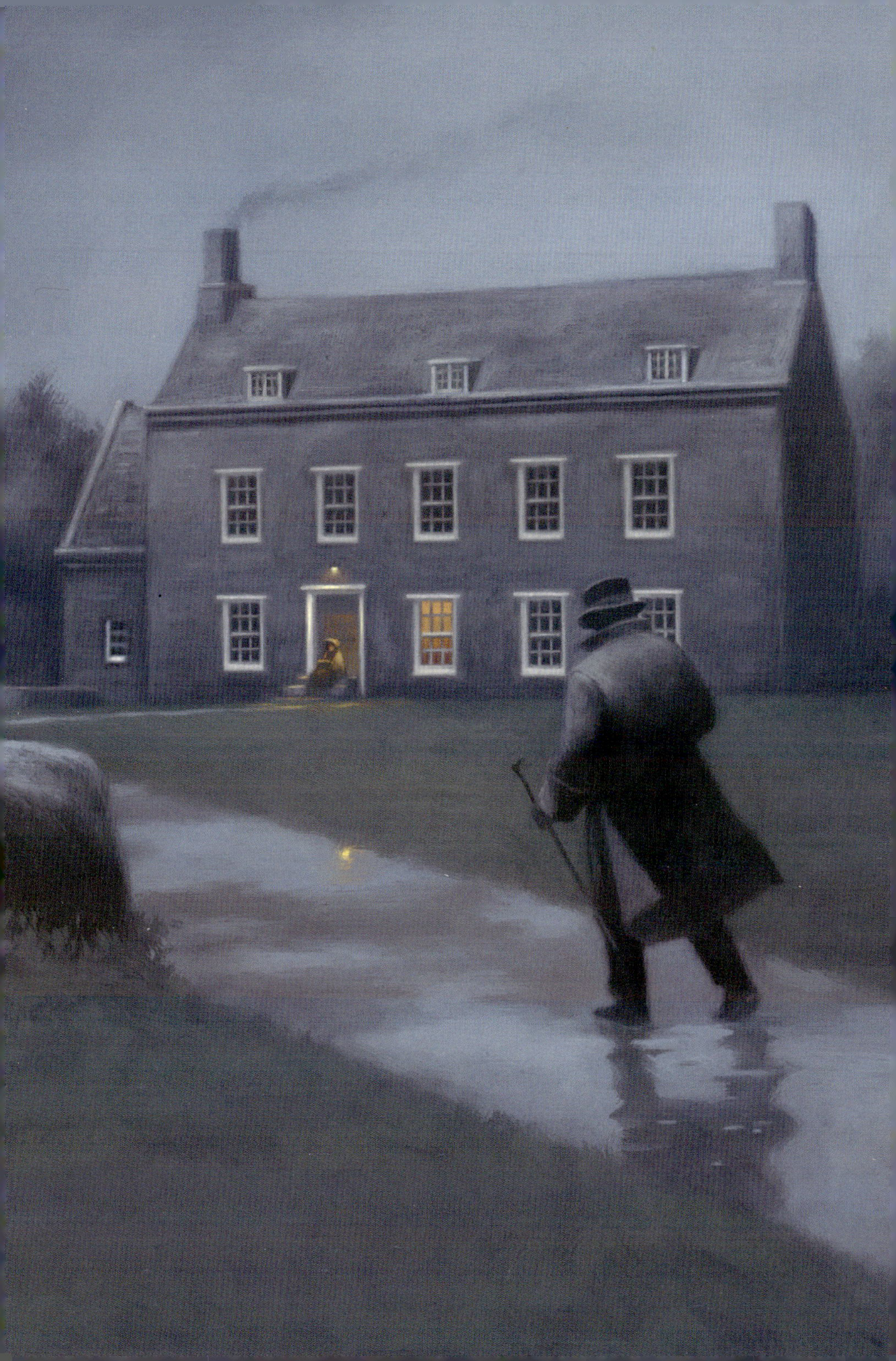

Jane Eyre

School and after I left I went to work as a governess. I had to leave suddenly, but I have done nothing wrong. Please believe me.'

'Don't worry, Jane, we believe you,' said Diana. 'Don't talk any more now. You are tired.'

'You will want to find some work,' said St John.

'Yes, and as soon as possible,' I replied.

'Good,' he said. 'Then I will help you.'

Diana and Mary went back to work at their teaching jobs in the south of England soon afterwards. St John asked me to teach the children who lived near his church. The school was very small and the children were very poor, but I enjoyed my work.

I lived in a small cottage near the school. I did not have much money, and I saw very few people, but St John often came to see me, and gave me books to read. My life was very quiet, but I was happy, except for when I thought about Mr Rochester. I knew that I would always love him.

ACTIVITIES

The text and **beyond**

1 Comprehension check

Put the sentences in the correct order to make a summary of Part Seven.

A ☐ The young man and his sisters looked after Jane because she was ill.
B ☐ The servant told Jane to go.
C ☐ Jane said that her name was Jane Elliott.
D ☐ Jane left Thornfield Hall.
E ☐ A young man found Jane on the doorstep.
F ☐ Jane knocked on the door of a house.
G ☐ Jane felt better and talked to the Rivers family.
H ☐ She still loved Mr Rochester.
I ☐ Jane taught children at the village school.
J ☐ Diana and Mary went back to their teaching jobs.

2 Find the mistake!

Here are some sentences from Part Seven, but each sentence contains a mistake. Correct them, then listen to Part Seven again to check your answers.

1 I wanted travel as far away from Thornfield as I could.
   ....
2 I arriving at a place where there were no towns or villages.
   ....
3 I thought that they looked kind, so I knock on the door.
   ....
4 'I'm alone in the world, and I have not money or food.'
   ....
5 I didn't know that someone was watching and listen to me.
   ....
6 The two young women asked me name.
   ....

83

ACTIVITIES

7 I was soon well enough to talk to the people who had been to me so kind.
....

8 The school was very small, and the children were very poor, but I enjoyed my working.
....

'My kind new friends took me upstairs to a bedroom, where I slept for a very long time'.

> Sometimes relative clauses with 'where' are an essential part of the sentence. They are 'defining relative clauses'. Without the relative clauses with 'where', these sentences are not complete.
> Look at these examples:
> *I saw the horrible school **where** Helen Burns died.*
> *India is **where** St John Rivers wanted to go.*
> Sometimes, though, relative clauses are not essential to the meaning of a sentence — they simply add extra information. Both the sentences below are complete and can still be understood without the relative clause. Notice too that these 'non-defining relative clauses' are separated from the main sentence by a comma or commas:
> *Helen Burns died in that old school, **where** Miss Temple taught French.*
> *India, **where** many other Englishmen worked, was the country of his dreams.*

3 Non-defining relative clauses with 'where'

Use the sentences in the box to make relative clauses with 'where' to put in the sentences (1-5). The new sentences must be true. There is an example at the beginning (0).

> Jane spent several sad years there with her horrible cousins.
> Mr Rochester lived there with his young bride.
> Mr Rochester hid his mad wife there.
> Mr Rochester's horse fell there.
> She went there to study French.
> Many little girls died of typhus there.

ACTIVITIES

0 Charlotte Brontë fell in love in Brussels, <u>where she went to study French</u>.

1 This road, ..., leads from Thornfield to the village.

2 That beautiful house, ..., belongs to Mrs Reed.

3 Jane went to work at Thornfield Hall, ...

4 Jane studied at Lowood school, ...

5 Mr Mason came from the West Indies, ...

4 Talking about Jane

The Rivers family were very surprised when Jane came to their house. Work in groups of three and pretend you are Mary, Diana and St John. Talk to each other about Jane. Here are some of the things you might discuss:

- Who is she?
- Where has she come from?
- Why is she alone?
- Why did she come to this house?

Compare your questions and answers with other groups.

For example: *Do you think that she's running away?*
Maybe she wants to start a new life.

T: GRADE 5

5 Speaking: health

1 When Jane was ill she slept for a long time, then felt better. What do you do when you feel ill?

2 How often do you visit the doctor? Why?

3 Do you prefer homeopathic or traditional medicine? Why?

85

ACTIVITIES

▶▶▶ INTERNET PROJECT ◀◀◀

Connect to the Internet and go to www.blackcat-cideb.com or www.cideb.it. Insert the title or part of the title of the book into our search engine. Open the page to *Jane Eyre*. Click on the Internet project link. Go down the page until you find the title of this book and click on the relevant link for this project.

There have been many film versions of *Jane Eyre*. There has even been a musical version of the novel.

Watch the videos of three of these versions and choose the one you like best, then present it to the class.

Say:
- why you liked it best;
- what scene or scenes are presented;
- when the film was made;
- who the actors and director are.

Before you read

1 Reading pictures

Look at the picture on page 89 and answer the questions.

1 Jane has a visitor. Who is it?
2 What do you think he is telling her?

PART **EIGHT**

Jane Makes a Choice

One evening, St John came to my house to see me when I was just finishing painting a picture. He looked closely at some of my other pictures. Then he tore a piece of paper off the bottom of one of the pictures and put it in his pocket. I waited for him to say something, but he remained silent. 'How strange he is,' I thought.

Even though it snowed the next day, and the weather was very cold, St John came to see me again. I was very surprised to see him.

'Why are you here?' I asked him. 'Has something bad happened? Are your sisters all right?'

'Don't worry,' he said. 'Diana and Mary are both well.'

St John sat down beside the fire and said nothing for a long time. I wondered[1] what had made him come to see me on such a cold, dark night.

1. **wondered**: asked myself.

Jane Eyre

At last, he spoke.

'Jane, I know your story,' he told me. 'I know about your parents, and Mrs Reed. I know about your time at Lowood and about Mr Rochester. I also know about Mr Rochester's wife. I know why you came here with no money. Mr Rochester must be a very bad man,' he said.

'No, no!' I cried. 'He isn't bad.'

'I have had a letter from a man in London, called Mr Briggs, who is looking for someone called Jane Eyre,' St John said. 'You say that your name is Jane Elliott, but I know that you are Jane Eyre. Look!' He showed me the piece of paper from the bottom of my painting. My real name, Jane Eyre, was on it.

'Does Mr Briggs know anything about Mr Rochester?' I asked. 'Does he know how Mr Rochester is?' I could only think about Mr Rochester, because I still loved him.

'Mr Briggs said nothing about Mr Rochester,' said St John. 'His letter was about your uncle, Mr Eyre of Madeira. Mr Eyre is dead. He left you all his money. You are very rich, Jane.'

I was so surprised that I was unable to speak for a long time. I did not feel excited or happy. Instead, I wondered what it would mean to be rich.

'I don't understand,' I said, when I was able to speak again. 'Why did Mr Briggs write to you?'

'Because,' said St John, 'Mr Eyre of Madeira was my mother's brother, which means that he is also our uncle.'

'Then you and your sisters are my cousins,' I said, feeling happy now. 'We can share the money between the four of us. Diana and Mary can come home, and we can all live together.'

It was good to have money, after being poor for all of my life, but it was even better to know that I had three cousins.

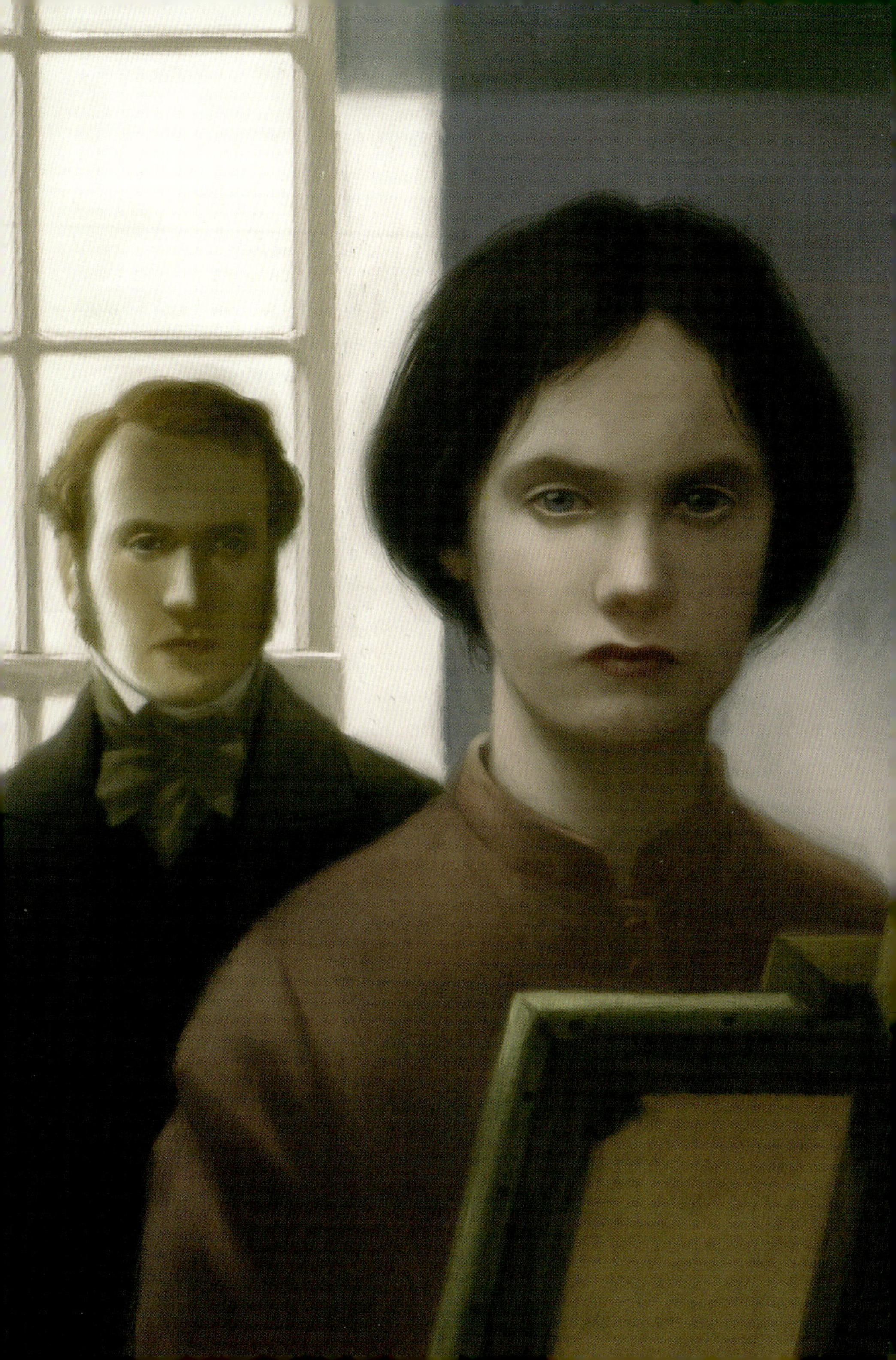

Jane Eyre

Diana and Mary came home just before Christmas. I worked happily to make their old house comfortable. 'I know that Diana and Mary will like it,' I thought. 'But what will St John think? He is such a strange man. He's hard and cold, like a stone. Even though he's pleased to see his sisters, he does not look really happy.'

I soon realised that St John was not content with just having money. He still wanted to go to India. I was happy living with Diana and Mary, but I still thought about Mr Rochester every day. Was he still at Thornfield? Was he happy? I had to know, so I wrote to the lawyer, Mr Briggs. Mr Briggs replied that he knew nothing about Mr Rochester. I wrote to Mrs Fairfax at Thornfield Hall, but there was no reply. When a letter came for me at last, it was from Mr Briggs about the money. I was so disappointed that I started to cry.

St John came into the room while I was crying. 'Jane, come for a walk with me,' he said. 'I want to talk to you.'

We walked together beside the river. St John was very quiet at first, but then he turned and said to me, 'Jane, I'm going to India soon, and I want you to come with me.'

I was very surprised by what he said. Why did he want me to go to India with him? How could I help him? I was not strong like he was.

'I don't think I would be a very good helper for you, St John…' I began to say.

'No, not as a helper. I want you to be my wife. If we get married, we can work together in India. There are many poor people there who need our help.'

It was hard to believe what St John was saying to me. I felt sure that he did not love me. I knew that I did not love him, and that I could not marry him. I still loved Mr Rochester.

Jane Makes a Choice

'I can't work in India. I don't know how to help the poor people there. I'm not like you, St John.'

'That doesn't matter,'[1] St John replied. 'I shall tell you what to do. You will soon learn. I saw how hard you worked in the village school. I know that you will work hard in India, too.'

I said nothing while I thought about what St John had said. He was my cousin and he needed my help. He was going to do good and useful work in India. Maybe I should do as he asked?

'If I help you, then I must be free,' I said. 'You are like a brother to me. I can't marry you.'

St John's face looked like stone. 'No, Jane, you must be my wife,' he said. 'I don't want a sister. I don't want you to marry another man. I want us to stay together and work together until we die.'

I turned away from St John so that he could not see how upset I was. I remembered my love for Mr Rochester. He had always been so kind and gentle when he spoke to me. St John spoke coldly to me, and I knew that he did not love me at all. He was a good man, but I knew that I would never love him. What could I say to him?

'I am going away for two weeks, to visit friends,' said St John. 'When I return, I will want to know your answer. I hope that you will agree to marry me. It is the right thing for you to do, Jane. You can't stay here forever, doing nothing.'

I saw Diana when I went back to the house. When she saw my unhappy face, she asked, 'What is wrong, Jane? You look so pale and upset. What has happened to you?'

---

1. **doesn't matter** : isn't important.

Jane Eyre

'St John has asked me to marry him,' I said, miserably.

'That is wonderful,' Diana cried. 'If you marry him, he will stay here in England with us, instead of going to India.'

'No,' I said. 'He wants me to go to India with him.'

Diana looked surprised. 'But you can't go to India,' she said. 'You're not strong[1] enough.'

'I won't go because I can't marry him,' I told her. 'I'm afraid that he's angry with me, Diana. I know that he's a good man, but I don't think that he understands how ordinary people feel.'

'Yes,' Diana said, seriously. 'My brother is a very good man, but sometimes he appears to be hard and cold.'

I lay awake in my bed that night, and I thought about St John. I could not decide what I should do. I knew that I did not love him, and I was sure that he did not love me. But maybe I should go to India? The night was very quiet. I could hear nothing in the darkness.

Suddenly, I thought that I heard a voice. 'Jane!' it called, 'Jane! Jane!'

It was Mr Rochester's voice.

'I am here, Mr Rochester.' I cried. 'Where are you? What is wrong?'

Was I dreaming? Perhaps, but it didn't matter. Somehow, I knew that Mr Rochester needed me. 'I must go to him at once,'[2] I thought.

The next day, I left once more for Thornfield Hall. It was a long journey, and I decided to walk for the last two miles to the house.

1. **strong** : (here) in good health.
2. **at once** : immediately.

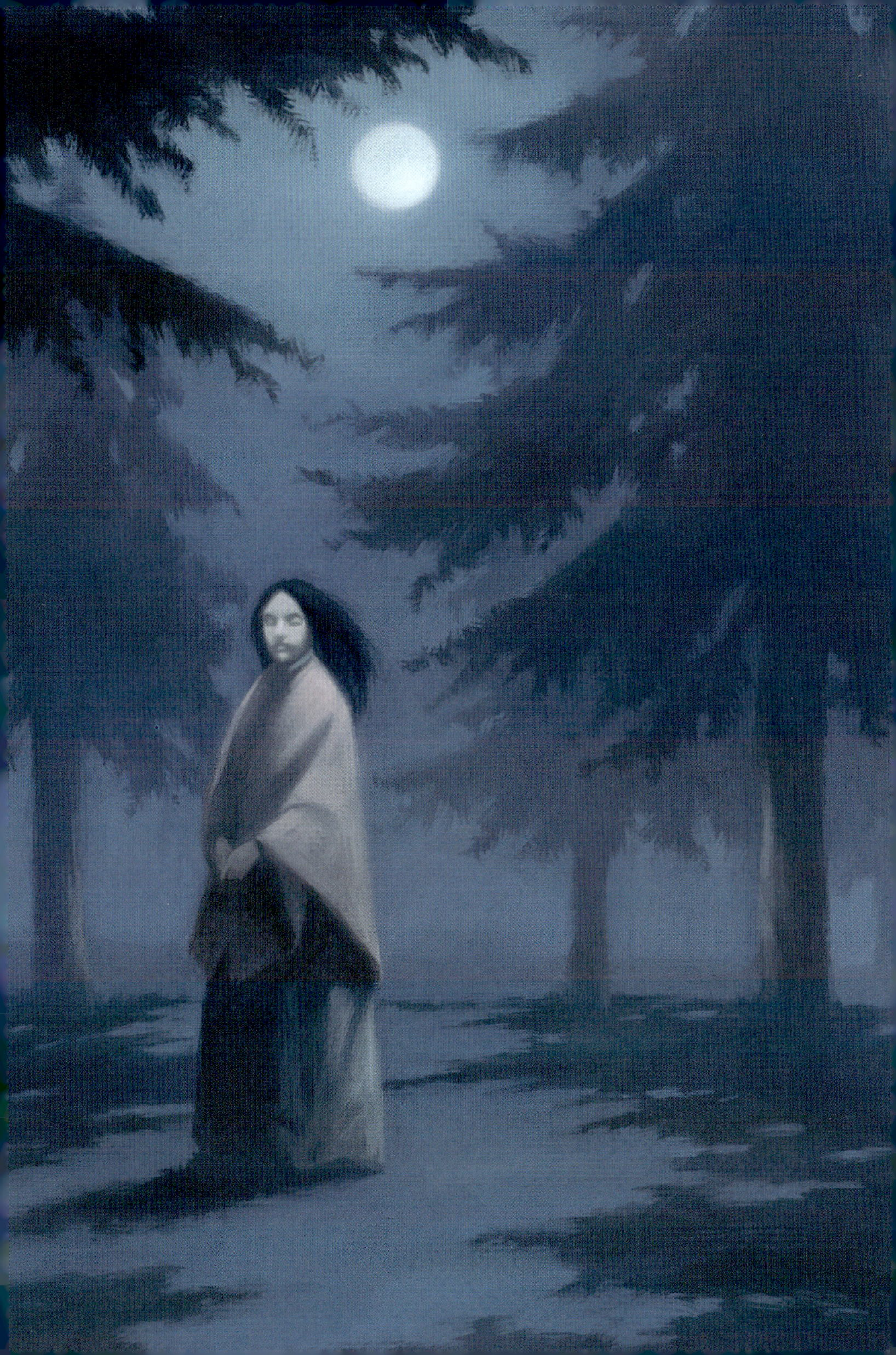

ACTIVITIES

The text and **beyond**

PET **1** **Comprehension check**

Read these sentences about Part Eight and decide if each sentence is correct or incorrect. If it is correct, mark A. If it is incorrect, mark B.

		A	B
1	St John went to see Jane to tell her that Diana was ill.	☐	☐
2	Jane didn't agree that Mr Rochester was a bad man.	☐	☐
3	Mr Briggs was looking for someone called Jane Eyre.	☐	☐
4	St John knew that Jane's real name was Jane Elliott.	☐	☐
5	Mr Briggs had left Jane all of his money.	☐	☐
6	Jane discovered that Mary, Diana and St John were her cousins.	☐	☐
7	Jane cried when she received a letter from Mr Rochester.	☐	☐
8	St John asked Jane to go to India with him.	☐	☐
9	Jane said she couldn't marry St John.	☐	☐
10	Jane thought she heard St John's voice in the night.	☐	☐
11	Next morning, Jane returned to Thornfield Hall.	☐	☐

Now correct the incorrect sentences.

2 **Discussion**

In Part Eight, Jane has to make some difficult decisions. Work with another student and take it in turns to answer the following questions about what you would do if you were Jane. Give reasons for your answers. Compare your answers with other students.

1. Would you share the money with your cousins, or would you keep it for yourself?
2. Would you agree to go to India with St John?
3. Would you go to India without St John?
4. Would you want to marry St John?
5. Would you go back to Thornfield Hall now ?
6. What would you do if you did not go back to Thornfield?

ACTIVITIES

3 Find the mistake!

The following sentences all contain a mistake. Rewrite them correctly.

1 ....: 'Why you are here? Has something bad happened?'
   ....

2 ....: 'I know why you came here with no moneys.'
   ....

3 ....: 'Mr Eyre was dead. He left you all his money.'
   ....

4 ....: 'Jane, coming for a walk with me.'
   ....

5 ....: 'What is right, Jane? You look so pale and upset.'
   ....

6 ....: 'My brother is very good man, but sometimes he appears to be hard and cold.'
   ....

7 ....: 'I am there, Mr Rochester.'
   ....

Can you write in the name of the person who said the words above? Check by listening to the recording.

T: GRADE 6

4 Speaking: money

1 Should all teenagers get pocket money?
2 Is it better to save or spend? Why?
3 Have prices gone up a lot recently in your country? If so, on what?

ACTIVITIES

PET 5 Fill in the gaps

Read this letter. Choose the correct word (A, B, C or D) to fill in each space.

> Dear Lizzie,
>
> I have (1) .... interesting news (2) .... you. A young woman is living with us. She (3) .... us that (4) .... name was Jane Elliott but we now know that she is called Jane Eyre.
>
> We all like Jane and my brother has asked her (5) .... marry him. I know that she likes St John, but I don't think that she wants to be his wife. I think that she may love (6) .... man.
>
> My brother wants Jane to go to India with him, he wishes to do his missionary work for his church there. However, I do not think that she is strong enough. She could not help him with the difficult work he will have in India. I wonder what (7) .... happen.
>
> Please (8) .... soon and tell me your news,
>
> Your friend,
> Diana

1	**A** any	**B** some	**C** an	**D** the
2	**A** for	**B** of	**C** by	**D** to
3	**A** tell	**B** tells	**C** told	**D** telling
4	**A** she	**B** he	**C** his	**D** her
5	**A** for	**B** too	**C** to	**D** and
6	**A** other	**B** a	**C** another	**D** the
7	**A** will	**B** going	**C** won't	**D** to
8	**A** write	**B** writes	**C** written	**D** wrote

ACTIVITIES

Before you read

1 Listening

Listen to the first part of Part Nine. For questions 1-6, choose the correct answer — A, B or C.

1 How did Jane feel about seeing Thornfield Hall?
 A ☐ very happy and agitated
 B ☐ very frightened and worried
 C ☐ very sad

2 Jane was told about the fire
 A ☐ by a man in the village.
 B ☐ by a man at the house.
 C ☐ by Mrs Fairfax.

3 The person responsible for the fire was
 A ☐ Mrs Fairfax
 B ☐ Mrs Rochester
 C ☐ Mr Rochester

4 Who died in the fire?
 A ☐ Mr Rochester
 B ☐ Mrs Rochester
 C ☐ some servants

5 The fire began
 A ☐ in the kitchen.
 B ☐ in a tree near the house.
 C ☐ in the attic.

6 Adèle was not hurt in the fire because
 A ☐ she was not home at the time.
 B ☐ she ran out quickly.
 C ☐ Mrs Fairfax saved her.

97

PART **NINE**

Return to Thornfield

I was so excited to think that I was going to see my old home again. The trees and the road were just the same as when I left. I arrived at the house, and stood and looked.

I could not believe what I saw. My beautiful home was in ruins! No one could live here now. I now knew why Mrs Fairfax never answered my letters. The walls of the house were still standing, but the roof had gone. The windows were dark and empty. The gardens were neglected.[1] The walls of the old house were black. There was no sound except for the song of birds and the noise of the wind. Where was Mrs Fairfax? Where was little Adèle? And where — oh where — was Mr Rochester?

I hurried back to the village and asked a man to tell me what had happened.

'Last autumn, the house burnt down in the middle of the night,' he told me.

---

1. **neglected** : not looked after.

Return to Thornfield

'How did it happen?' I asked him.

'People say that Mr Rochester's wife started the fire,' he said. 'No one ever saw the lady, but they say that she was mad. They say she started the fire in the attic, where she lived. Mrs Fairfax was visiting friends when it happened, and the little girl, Adèle, was away at school.'

I stared at the man. I could not believe what he was telling me.

'Mr Rochester didn't want to see anyone at the time,' he said. 'It seems he was very unhappy. He wanted to marry a young girl, but she ran away.'

'What happened when the fire started?' I asked.

'Mr Rochester got all the servants out of the house,' he continued, 'and then he went back in to save his wife. I saw her standing on the roof. She was waving [1] her arms and shouting. Mr Rochester tried to help her, but she would not let him. Suddenly she fell from the roof.'

'Did she die?' I asked.

'Yes, she died at once,' he said. 'And Mr Rochester was badly injured. When he came out of the house, he was blind and he had lost one hand.'

I had been so afraid that the man was going to tell me that Mr Rochester was dead. I began to hope again. He was hurt, but he was still alive!

'Where does Mr Rochester live now?' I asked the man.

'He lives near here, at a quiet little place called Ferndean,' he replied. 'He can't travel far since he was hurt. He lives with just two servants. He never has any visitors.'

I went to Ferndean at once, and arrived there just before

---

1. **waving** : moving her arms quickly.

Jane Eyre

dark. When I got near the house, I saw a man come out. I knew at once that it was Mr Rochester. He looked so different from the man I had known. He was still tall and his hair was still dark, but his face was sad. He could not walk without help. After a few minutes, he turned and went slowly back into the house.

I knocked on the door and Mary, a servant, answered it. She recognised me [1] at once. I told her that I had heard about the fire at Thornfield Hall, and about what had happened to Mr Rochester.

'Go to Mr Rochester and tell him that he has a visitor,' I said to Mary. 'But don't tell him who it is.'

'He won't see you, Miss Jane,' she said. 'He has refused to see anyone since the fire.'

I went into the room where Mr Rochester was sitting.

'Is that you, Mary?' he asked. 'Answer me!'

'Will you have some water?' I said to him.

'That is Jane Eyre's voice,' Mr Rochester said. 'Jane, is it really you?'

'Yes. It is really me,' I said. 'I've come home to be with you. I'll never leave you again.'

'Oh Jane, why did you go?' he asked. 'Why did you leave so suddenly? Why did you not stay and let me help you?'

'You know why I went,' I said. 'It was the only thing that I could do. But things have changed. I am a rich woman now.'

I told Mr Rochester all about my cousins, and about my new home.

'Then you do not need me now,' he said. 'Will you really stay with me?' There was hope in his voice. I smiled at him, although he could not see me.

'Of course I will,' I said.

'But you're so young,' he said. 'You don't want to marry me.

---

1. **recognised me** : knew who I was.

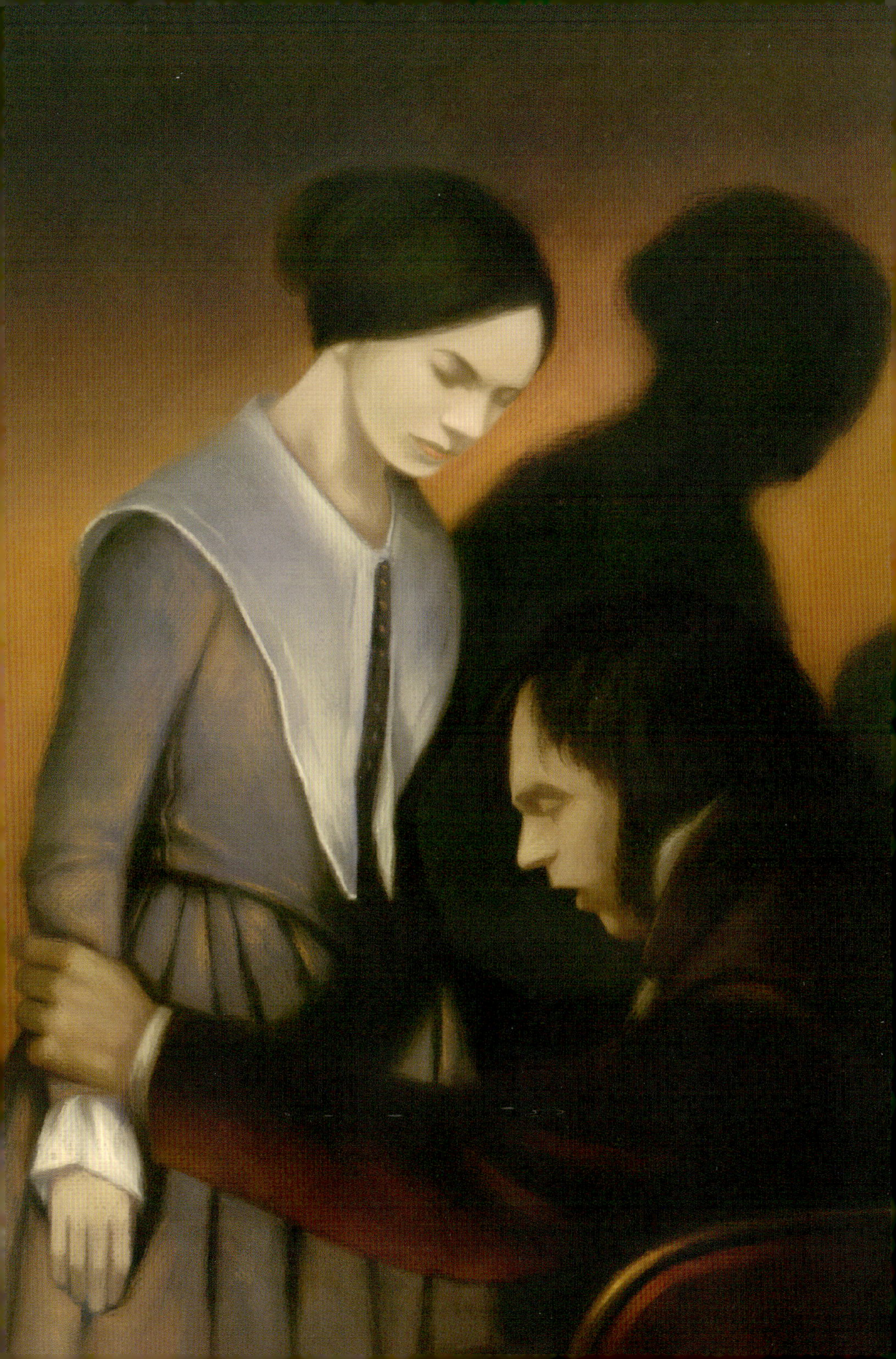

Jane Eyre

I'm blind and I can't do anything. You must marry a young man. What is your cousin, St John Rivers, like? Is he young or old?'

'He is young and handsome,' I answered.

'Do you like him?' he asked.

'Yes, I do,' I answered. 'He's a very good man.'

'Does he like you?' he asked.

'Yes, he does,' I answered. 'He wants me to marry him.'

'Will you marry him?' he asked.

'No. I don't love him.' I told him.

Mr Rochester looked happy. He held my hand, and he was silent for a long time. Then, at last he said to me very quietly, 'Jane, may I ask you again now? Will you marry me?'

'Yes, I will marry you,' I said. I was delighted. Mr Rochester, too, looked happier than I had ever seen him.

Three days later, Mr Rochester and I were married.

Diana and Mary were delighted when I wrote to tell them the news. I also wrote to St John, but he never replied. He went to India and did much good work there, but he never married.

Little Adèle came back to live with us when she had finished school. She is now a wonderful friend to me.

Mr Rochester and I have now been married for ten years. Two years after we were married, Mr Rochester began to see again with one eye. He can now see me and our two children.

Our story has been a strange and terrible one. We both suffered [1] greatly before we could be together, but now, at last, we are happy.

1. **suffered** : had difficult experiences.

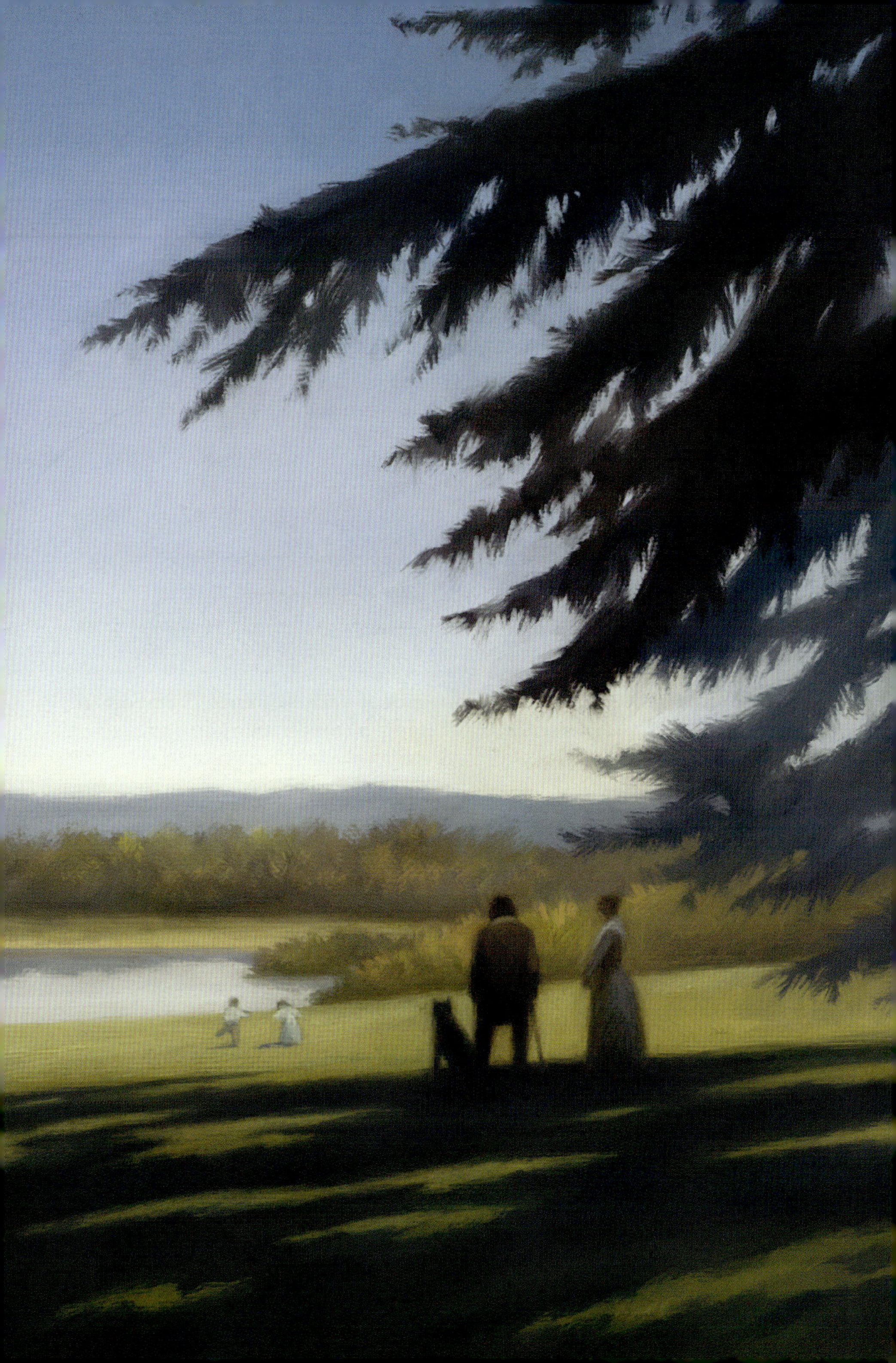

ACTIVITIES

The text and **beyond**

1 Comprehension check
Answer the following questions.

1 Why could Jane not believe what she saw when she returned to Thornfield?
2 Who told Jane what had happened while she was away?
3 Who did the man think had started the fire?
4 How did Mr Rochester's wife die?
5 What happened to Mr Rochester?
6 When Jane saw Mr Rochester, how had he changed?
7 What was the first question that Jane asked Mr Rochester?
8 What was the first question that Mr Rochester asked Jane?
9 Who did Mr Rochester say that Jane should marry?
10 What happened at the end of the story?

PET 2 Read the sentences below and decide if each sentence is correct or incorrect. If it is correct, mark A. If it is incorrect, mark B.

		A	B
1	Jane was worried about seeing Thornfield Hall again.	☐	☐
2	Mrs Fairfax told her what had happened to Mr Rochester.	☐	☐
3	Mr Rochester tried to help his wife.	☐	☐
4	A stranger opened the door to Jane.	☐	☐
5	Mary told Jane that Mr Rochester would be pleased to see her.	☐	☐
6	Jane told Mr Rochester about her new life.	☐	☐
7	Mr Rochester didn't want to marry Jane.	☐	☐
8	Jane and Mr Rochester had three children and Adèle went to live with them.	☐	☐

Now correct the incorrect sentences.

ACTIVITIES

3 Verbs
In the following sentences, put the verbs in the brackets in the correct tense.

1 I was so excited to think I .... (*go*) to visit my old friends again.
2 Finally I .... (*know*) why Mrs Fairfax never answered my letters.
3 'The house .... (*burn*) down in the middle of the night last summer.'
4 '........................... (*he/want*) to marry a young girl?'
5 'She .... (*stand*) on the roof.'
6 'He .... (*refuse*) to see anyone since the fire.'
7 After she .... (*finish*) school little Adèle came back to live with us.
8 Do you think our story .... (*have*) been a strange and terrible one?

4 A film
In groups, imagine you are making a film of *Jane Eyre*. Which actors would you use to play the characters in the story? Why? Compare your answers with the other groups.

5 Another ending
Write another ending to the story (about 100 words). Compare your ideas with other students.

6 Jane Eyre
Many people think that Jane Eyre is a strong character. What do you think? Give some examples that justify your opinion. Discuss this with your partner and then present your ideas to the class.

Victorian Houses

Houses are important in *Jane Eyre*. First of all Jane lived at Mrs Reed's house, which she said was 'large and beautiful'. The next house that she lived in was Thornfield Hall. Jane loved living at Thornfield, and she was very sad when she returned in the last part of the story and discovered that it was in ruins.

When Jane left Thornfield, she lived at St John and his sisters' house. Jane does not describe it, but we can imagine that it was much smaller than either Mrs Reed's house or Thornfield Hall. The house near the school where Jane lived while she taught was a small cottage.

Haworth Parsonage, built in 1778-89, became the home of Patrick Brontë, his wife Maria and their six children. Today it is a museum; you can also make a virtual visit on the Internet.

A drawing room.

What did a Victorian house look like? If the owner had a lot of money, the house was very comfortable. Houses in pleasant parts of cities were often built in terraces. [1] They might have three floors and a large cellar. [2] There were gardens at the front and back.

On the ground floor was a dining room, where the family ate their meals. There was a drawing room, where people sat in the evening and played cards or listened to music. Victorian families liked to sing together. At the back of the house or in the basement was the kitchen and scullery, [3] where the washing up was done. Big houses had breakfast rooms, studies and sometimes libraries.

The bedrooms and nursery [4] were on the first floor. The servants

1. **terraces** : rows of houses.
2. **cellar** : room under the house.
3. **scullery** : little room next to a kitchen.
4. **nursery** : room where small children play and sleep.

A bedroom.

lived in the attics at the top of the house. The dining room had a large central table surrounded by wooden straight-backed chairs. The father of the house sat at the top end of the table. He cut up the meat for the rest of the family at mealtimes. The drawing room or parlour had leather armchairs, a sofa, sideboards [1] and maybe a grandfather clock. [2]

The rooms had open fireplaces. The beds were warmed at night with a stone bottle filled with hot water. Because few people had bathrooms, people washed in the bedrooms. There was a washstand in each bedroom with a large jug and basin. When the family had baths, a servant carried a small bath to the bedroom. She filled it with hot water which had to be brought up from the kitchen. Rich people usually had an indoor toilet, but in poorer people's houses the toilet was outside.

Cottages were very simple. Sometimes there was just one room

1. **sideboards** : pieces of furniture with cupboards, drawers and shelves.
2. **grandfather clock** : clock in a long case which stands on the floor.

108

downstairs, which was both a kitchen and living room, and a bedroom upstairs. The floor was made of stone, with no carpet in poorer homes. The water was brought from a pump or well [1] outside.

1 A Victorian house

Use the text on pages 106-108 to help you name the rooms.

1 ....
2 ....
3 ....
4 ....
5 ....
6 ....
7 ....
8 ....
9 ....
10 ....
11 ....

2 Reading pictures

Look at the pictures on pages 107-108 and talk about these questions.

1 What are the biggest similarities and differences between the rooms in the pictures and rooms in your home?
2 What elements of the rooms do you think are typically Victorian? What elements do you like/dislike?

1. **well** : deep hole in the ground from which people get water.

AFTER READING

1 Comprehension check

Did you enjoy *Jane Eyre*? Here is a quiz about the story. Answer the questions.

1   What was the name of Jane's aunt?
2   What was the name of Jane's school?
3   Who was Jane's male cousin?
4   Who was her best friend at school?
5   What was Jane's student's name?
6   What did Jane hear and smell very early one morning?
7   Who lived in the attic?
8   Who said, 'Stop the wedding'?
9   Who took Jane in when she was cold, tired and hungry?
10 Where did Jane work when she recovered from her illness?
11 What made Jane go back to Thornfield Hall?
12 What was the name of the servant who let Jane into Mr Rochester's house?
13 How long after Jane's return were she and Mr Rochester married?
14 How long had Jane been married to Mr Rochester at the end of the story?

2 Picture summary

Look at the pictures. Put them in the order in which they appear in the novel.

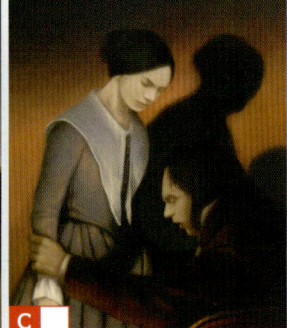

A   B   C

AFTER READING

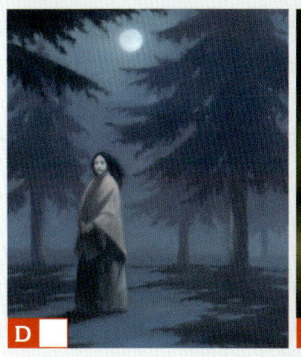

D E F

G H I

3 **A graphic novel**

Photocopy these two pages, cut out the pictures and stick them on paper in the right order. Think of words to put in the balloons when the characters are speaking or thinking. Do not use the words that were used in this book! Then write at least a sentence under each picture to narrate what is happening.

4 **Writing**

Imagine you are Jane and are recording the most important event of your life in your diary. Write 120-180 words.

This reader uses the **EXPANSIVE READING** approach, where the text becomes a springboard to improve language skills and to explore historical background, cultural connections and other topics suggested by the text.

The new structures introduced in this step of our **READING & TRAINING** series are listed below. Naturally, structures from lower steps are included too. For a complete list of structures used over all the six steps, see *Black Cat Guide to Graded Readers*, which is also downloadable at no cost from our website, www.blackcat-cideb.com or www.cideb.it.

The vocabulary used at each step is carefully checked against vocabulary lists used for internationally recognised examinations.

Step Three B1.2

All the structures used in the previous levels, plus the following:

Verb tenses
Present Perfect Simple: unfinished past with
   for or *since* (duration form)
Past Perfect Simple: narrative

Verb forms and patterns
Regular verbs and all irregular verbs in current
   English
Causative: *have / get* + object + past participle
Reported questions and orders with *ask* and *tell*

Modal verbs
Would: hypothesis
Would rather: preference
Should (present and future reference):
   moral obligation
Ought to (present and future reference):
   moral obligation
Used to: past habits and states

Types of clause
2nd Conditional: *if* + past, *would(n't)*
Zero, 1st and 2nd conditionals with *unless*
Non-defining relative clauses with *who*
   and *where*
Clauses of result: *so*; *so ... that*; *such ... that*
Clauses of concession: *although*, *though*

Other
Comparison: *(not) as / so ... as*; *(not) ...*
   enough to; *too ... to*

Available at Step Three:

- **The £1,000,000 Bank Note** Mark Twain
- **Alien at School** Michelle Brown
- **Bizarre Tales** Peter Foreman
- **The Canterville Ghost** Oscar Wilde
- **Classic Detective Stories**
- **The Diamond as Big as The Ritz**
  F. Scott Fitzgerald
- **Duck Soup** Peter Foreman
- **Great Mysteries of Our World**
  Gina D. B. Clemen
- **Gulliver's Travels** Jonathan Swift
- **The Hound of the Baskervilles**
  Sir Arthur Conan Doyle
- **Jane Eyre** Charlotte Brontë
- **Julius Caesar** William Shakespeare
- **Lord Arthur Savile's Crime**
  and Other Stories Oscar Wilde
- **Of Mice and Men** John Steinbeck
- **The Pearl** John Steinbeck
- **The Phantom of the Opera** Gaston Leroux
- **The Prisoner of Zenda** Anthony Hope
- **The Red Badge of Courage** Stephen Crane
- **The Return of Sherlock Holmes**
  Sir Arthur Conan Doyle
- **Romeo and Juliet** William Shakespeare
- **The Scarlet Pimpernel** Baroness Orczy
- **Sherlock Holmes Investigates**
  Sir Arthur Conan Doyle
- **Stories of Suspense** Nathaniel Hawthorne
- **The Strange Case of Dr Jekyll and Mr Hyde**
  Robert Louis Stevenson
- **Tales of the Supernatural**
- **Three Men in a Boat** Jerome K. Jerome
- **Treasure Island** Robert Louis Stevenson
- **Twelfth Night** William Shakespeare
- **The Vegas Hills Carnival Mystery**
  Michelle Brown